ACORD Web site: http://www.acord.org

FIRST EDITION

Design: Oxygen Design

ISBN 0-9768967-0-2

The Business Information REVOLUTION

Making the Case for ACORD Standards

Gregory A. Maciag

President & CEO

"There are people (both staff and volunteers) too numerous to mention whose contributions over my 28 years at ACORD have led to the ideas and opinions I voiced in the pages of this book. But there are no more important people in my life today who continue to support and nurture my passion for ACORD than my wife Carol and my daughter Michelle. The success I have been fortunate enough to achieve has only been possible because they have understood the personal commitment necessary in the work that I do. For their unwavering love and support, I dedicate this book to my wife and daughter."

— Gregory Maciag

Greetings! I am sure you readily accept the need for standards. I know that because if we talked about how standards make everything in life possible, there would be no argument between us.

But I am also sure that you seldom if ever think about standards. That is unless you get caught up in many of life's situations where standards or the lack of them becomes personal. Whether it's connecting home devices, calling through cell phone networks or whenever things don't fit or work together very well. I am using Standards at this very moment by communicating with you using a shared language, vocabulary and grammar known as English. If we spoke a few different languages, we'd have problems. If we all spoke a different language, we would have chaos.

The problem is that we do not easily transfer our thinking and understanding of Standards to the emerging information-based business world. Aside from weights and measures or engineering tolerances, data or information Standards appear to be something rather optional. But keep two points in mind: (1) What you did in the past will not carry you into a very different future; and (2) the price of not using Standards will continue to rise exponentially.

Lastly, let's be candid about the reasons why data Standards may not have been a high priority in your business in the past. First, all the costs of not using Standards are not obvious to everyone. Second, people make money (employees and suppliers) from the status quo and are not motivated to change. Third, Standards get caught up in the skeptical attitudes about IT in general rather than as a solution to IT shortfalls. And fourth, Standards are a long term strategy confronted with short term thinking.

Today, no one can write off data incompatibilities as merely another cost of doing business passed along to the customer. Today, information is an integral part of our business, all business for that matter. And Standards are intended to bring down the (systems, networks and technology) barriers to open trade. The absence of Standards will not be an option in the future. So we are on a journey and I need your help. It requires a small investment of time and money. It requires some attention to what we are doing and where we are going. And it requires a sense of commitment that only a long term and top down strategy can provide. The benefits are not only lower costs and access to markets, but ultimately, the ability to do business at all.

Who Should Read This Book

- CEOs and board members who want to raise their business's sights to new kinds of markets, partners, channels and products and who are looking to recast their investments in information resources as primary business variables.

- CIOs and other senior technology managers who want to improve the robustness and openness of their information architectures, enhance their ability to adapt to changes in business requirements, and to turn technology potential into real bottom-line business benefits.

- Technologists seeking a wider business context for their work in standards-based systems integration.

- ACORD participants seeking an industry and business context for their work in standards-building, advocacy and implementation.

The Business Information REVOLUTION

Making the Case for ACORD Standards

Gregory A. Maciag

President & CEO

Table of Contents

Prologue

I'VE SPENT ALL OF MY PROFESSIONAL LIFE in the insurance business. When I count up the years, I realize I've devoted the majority of my time in the business to helming ACORD, the business standards organization set up by the industry in the 1970s with the express purpose of making insurance business easier to do. We've come a long way. We've learned a lot, and achieved a lot. And of course, as the industry continues to grow and change, there's plenty more to do.

At the time of this writing I'm dividing my time between New York and London. The progress being made in London toward an open, highly efficient and flexible insurance market that confirms London's position as a leading world player is truly remarkable. There's a quiet revolution underway in London, and its manifesto is standards. This book culminates in a chapter on London and its role as a signpost to the future of the industry. But what's happening in London is an illustration of a truth we in the ACORD community see every day, in companies large and small. Organizations everywhere are reaping benefits from the power of standards. Standards are saving companies, creating new markets and serving customers better.

Collaborate or Die

> "Standards formally capture the structure of the information the industry needs to transact, transform, share and audit."

So it's worth taking a moment to reflect on the standards movement and asking where it came from, and what's behind it. First, standards are a means of an industry combining and collaborating around better ways of working. That's why ACORD is a community organization, and why we are not aligned with any regulator, or technology vendor, or other external influence. Standards formally capture the structure of the information the industry, as a body of interested parties, needs to transact, transform, share and audit. They're the "what" of the business we do every day. That's why I say ACORD is not a technology organization, but a business effectiveness organization.

Second, ACORD and its deliverables are an expression of the community's urge to grow. Connectivity – in the form of fixed or wireless networks and the plethora of devices and systems that can be attached to them – creates the potential for novel forms of commercial collaboration, product and service delivery and indeed product and service design. But physical connectivity is only a *potential* benefit. We need to turn wires into business pathways. And this is a huge part of ACORD's role. Standards can deliver internal efficiencies, but they have even greater value in opening up new pathways to commercial creativity – on a global scale.

> **"We need to turn wires into business pathways."**

In a lifetime of working the interface between business and IT, I've fielded a ton of boundary issues. I've seen the first wave of value added networks briefly become the tail that wagged the business dog. I've also seen the backlash, with the network suppliers treated as commodity suppliers and the technologists forced to make every systems project stand up to a solid business case. And as the business/IT dividing line has shifted – sometimes resembling a battlefront – the line has become increasingly blurred. Business folks are now computer literate: and technologists who argue that "users" don't know how to program are missing the point that they are now extremely well equipped to articulate their requirements of technology. IT folks are now more business-savvy, and during the 1990s saw their industry lead the business community in terms of financial, construction and delivery innovation. As the waves of evolution sweep back and forth along the beach, the line in the sand is washed away each time. It's time we stopped pretending we need that line.

The Power of Networks

Standards are the single most important vehicle in the removal of the old dividing line between the business and IT. Standards such as ACORD's encapsulate the DNA of the business and make it available to IT systems. And standards are developed, governed and transmitted by dedicated professionals from the businesses they serve. ACORD's role as an eraser of the artificial business/IT divide is, I believe, inevitable given the interaction of contemporary technology and business practice at a wider scale. Boundaries are falling wherever we look. Bank customers drive their own bank accounts via the PC. Supermarket customers instruct the entire grocery supply chain to deliver the weekly food order to their door. Companies construct and dissolve working alliances around the world and around the clock, using the power of the network to link resources with a flexibility and efficiency we could not dream of even ten years ago. The old walls have tumbled and an infinite number of new relationships have become possible. Standards enable organizations to discount the boundaries that have traditionally constrained their ambitions, and to exploit the possibilities of a world that's now effectively open for business.

I believe information technology is an engine of business evolution. Harnessing this engine is down to mindset. Those who succeed with information technology do so because they focus on the "information" part, not the "technology" part. They have the resolve to articulate their strategies, communicate with their partners, and influence the environment within which they operate. And this is exactly what ACORD does. We articulate the current and future needs of the community, express those findings in a way that's accessible to people and systems alike, and release our deliverables into the world to add enduring bottom-line value.

Organizations Have Fewer Boundaries

Some business writers have expressed the opinion that IT doesn't need creative management. In their view, IT is a cost of doing business and shouldn't be privileged above any other business function. And I agree. Technology isn't the point. But business information – that's the wealth

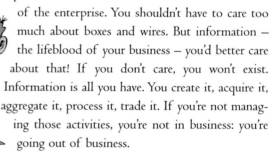

of the enterprise. You shouldn't have to care too much about boxes and wires. But information – the lifeblood of your business – you'd better care about that! If you don't care, you won't exist. Information is all you have. You create it, acquire it, aggregate it, process it, trade it. If you're not managing those activities, you're not in business: you're going out of business.

In the days when information was just a concern limited to the organization's own administrative domain, the efficiency and effectiveness of information management were not highly visible measures. But today, business bleeds over the boundaries of organizations. We work together on behalf of our clients. We exchange information with each other, and create new opportunities together. Being an isolated player simply isn't an option any more. The rules have changed. Today's insurance industry is precisely about connectivity, because it's concerned with creating new offers that mobilize wider sets of expert players and reach deeper into markets. The industry is competitive, sure: but it's also cooperative.

A Business Information Revolution

The first few chapters in the book look at us, as committed business people, securing, purifying and cir-culating the lifeblood of the insur-ance industry: information.

It's not primarily about technology, although technology plays a big part in the story. Nor is it about the low-level detail of data and process, although those details are the most visible and practical items that ACORD produces on behalf of the industry.

Our focus is not on the details, but on the fundamentals. This book establishes the promi-nent role of standards in *all* successful industries and markets. It lays bare the real, enduring economic actuality of our net-worked world and its ever-advancing technological capabilities. And it shows how all the players in the insurance industry – from underwriters to customers, via software vendors and media commentators – must combine and collaborate around better ways of getting work done.

The insurance industry has a long and fascinating history. But it has an equally exciting – if not more exciting – future. The great days are ahead of us. Smart organizations and smart business leaders are already beginning to enjoy the benefits and enhanced opportunities that standards-based data exchange brings. This book will show you how you can join the leaders.

Standards Are Essential

Business information standards are the single most important issue in contemporary management. Without standards, there's no genuine connectivity, there's just spaghetti. Without standards, there's no transparency to your business processes, just shadows where error and fraud can breed. Without standards, managers aren't managing: they're praying.

> **"Without standards, there's no genuine connectivity, there's just spaghetti."**

The business information revolution is upon us. It's a revolution of our own making, a product of our own collective will. Business wants business to be better: to be more profitable, more accountable and more creative. Information is the precious resource that is driving our progress. The confident, careful management of this resource through its lifecycle sorts the winners from the losers. And in our highly connected world, membership of the standards-using community has become the ticket to the game. If you're not using standards, then you're gone.

The future unfolding around us is one of immense opportunity. ACORD has been leading the way toward ever more reliable, value-adding and opportunity-creating information exchange for 35 years. If you'd like a quick history of where ACORD came from, jump to the last chapter and see how we got here. We have the road map for the future, and as the world's most mature and committed business information standards community, we are proud to offer our companionship for the journey ahead.

Enjoy this book.

Scribble on it. Rip it up—rip it off.

Throw it at your colleagues.

Take what you need from it.

Call me and *let's talk* about it.

This is *your* revolution.

GAM

1

The Connected World

Sorting the dotcom hype from the reality of the new Internet era

Despite the upheavals in the stock markets, and the discredited claims of some pioneers and pundits, the Internet has enormous potential to change our enterprises. We've passed the Bubble historically. Now we just need to get over it.

In this chapter I look at how the key elements of the age of Internet hype played out in reality, and the messages those developments have for business. I introduce a wave model of technology's impact on the economy, showing we've been through these upheavals many times before — and will do so again in the future. Finally I look for the source of stability, reliability and progression in times of great change — and find it in the products of standards-building communities.

Hype And Reality

What was it all about? Well, the dotcom Bubble taught us a few valuable lessons. We know it wasn't a pure technology story, but a situation caused by a confluence of technological, financial and social factors. We learned the financial markets can be misleading and Wall Street does not necessarily reflect Main Street. We're beginning to learn an extended period of "irrational exuberance" can also be a good time to hide poor judgment and ethical standards.

Hype vs Reality

> *"The net changes everything..."*
>
> *"...but change is unpredictable and discontinuous."*
>
> *"You've got to have first-mover advantage..."*
>
> *"...but first movers face huge risks."*
>
> *"What can be disintermediated will be disintermediated..."*
>
> *"...but much will be reintermediated."*
>
> *"I'm a millionaire now, so I must be right..."*
>
> *"...but if you're so rich, how come you ain't smart?"*

We also learned good ideas still need infrastructure to deliver on the vision. Many of the Bubble era's best ideas remain good ideas, even though their promoters have largely failed to make them scale in the market. It's clear, future success will come to those with their feet squarely planted on the ground and business models that generate revenues and/or reduce costs. Now the period of hype is over, it's easier to get a better handle on the reality of the net's contribution to the future of business.

"Good ideas still need infrastructure to deliver on the vision."

Pundits liked to tell us "the net changes everything," the economic cycle had broken through into "the long boom," and those who "didn't get it" would be left in the dust. It's true the net has changed our world, but it has not changed our deep-seated reactions to change. Just because something is possible, doesn't mean it is historically inevitable.

This fallacy – that the logic of a technology development will revolutionize human institutions, habits and economic models overnight – is the motive force behind each element of net hype. If you see historical inevitability in the deployment of a new channel, then naturally you will seize on "first-mover advantage" as a benefit. Yet rational reflection tells us pioneers also suffer and die in their efforts to colonize new ground. Making a radical change in your business model is not something to be undertaken lightly, or under the imagined pressure of acute competitive activity. Did we really believe the business cycle had shrunk to "Internet time," and there was no compensating danger for those who lived at that speed?

Disintermediation

The fallacy of global disintermediation perhaps has a more illustrious source in economic theory. Yet, as we shall see in the next chapter, just because an intermediary can be removed, it doesn't mean their removal will confer any benefits on the transacting parties. It's all too easy to assume intermediaries are parasites in the market, rather than being the business connectors that give the market its liquidity.

Finally, it's worth remembering much of the Bubble era hype was simply that: rhetoric. It was windy talk that helped to sell magazines. When your mother told you about the wonders of the coming Internet century, you felt edgy. But when some paper-millionaire fresh from his NASDAQ listing told us the way it was going to be, we respected his millions. I've met enough smiling dotcom "millionaires" and heard them laugh at their brief, unrealizable fortunes to know it was only a small minority who let their sudden wealth convince them they had the Midas touch. But it was this minority of voices we heard amplified in the media.

The gas has gone out of the Bubble, leaving us to consider the true, enduring effects of the net. Yes, the markets went crazy, logic went out the window and our 401Ks may be worth a bit less as a result. But connected networks (with ACORD industry standards) offer promising potential for our business. Competitive advantage is now more than ever based on open systems, self-service applications, alliances and the sharing of information among suppliers, distributors and customers. Legacy and proprietary systems may not disappear overnight, but middleware and customer-facing applications are becoming overwhelmingly open and standards-centric. In fact, standards are no longer expedient, but crucial to the goal of openness.

> **"Competitive advantage is now more than ever based on open systems."**

ACORD facilitates collaboration and promotes competition among the suppliers of software and services to insurers and agencies. Equally important, through industry standards we cultivate an open environment that allows everyone to reach beyond the enterprise and simplify the way trading partners conduct business. This is not going to be easy, nor is it going to happen overnight. We will need to continue working together as an industry to achieve it. That's the reality.

Not Hyped Enough

Believe it or not, the stock market chaos in the technology sector, and the outbreak of Enronitis that followed it, has obscured some very real Internet successes. Those successes combined technology, standards, a network and a business model that created "real" business value and opportunity such as *E-bay*®, *Google*™, and *Yahoo*®. Here are two more key developments you won't read about in the papers:

Commoditization of complex goods and services

Consumer ecommerce has been particularly successful in retailing some complex products and services directly to consumers, reducing costs to customers and squeezing intermediaries — or forcing them to focus on value-add. The leading examples are books, music and air travel. The online success of these sectors contrasts markedly with the pundits' vision for the Internet, which was one of digital texts and virtual reality. We've used the new channel to revolutionize existing businesses. But that's not sexy enough for a magazine article.

Interoperability of business-to-business systems

The net and business standards frameworks like XML (which can be used to embody ACORD standards) allow businesses to connect with each other at the operational level. Business portals and extranets have revolutionized the relationships between business partners, enhancing their value chains and helping them to share their missions like never before. Deep-level business-to-business collaboration dispenses with human operator intervention. There's no website to show, and no day-to-day human angle — so it doesn't make the papers.

It's Happened Before

We've been here before, as Tom Standage chronicles in *The Victorian Internet* [1]. Standage explores the invention of the telegraph in the 19th century, drawing parallels between the telegraph and the Internet. Considering messages traveled by horse and boats in those days, a telegraph network that could send messages across long distances in minutes was indeed a revolution. He closes by saying if Victorians arrived today, they would be impressed by our heavier-than-air flying machines and space travel. But as for the Internet, they would say: "We had one of our own."

Perhaps the most revealing and resonant point of Standage's book is people do not change as fast as technology. I have heard Bill Gates say repeatedly we tend to over-estimate the short term but under-estimate the long term.

The crude telegraph has had a profound effect upon us all through the years. It gave birth to many other inventions, including the telephone, fax and the Internet, and it inspired many new ways of doing business. Unlike the telegraph, the ubiquity of the net means every human on earth can be connected today. And this connectivity requires the same agreement on standards as the telegraph did in the 19th century.

Without standard protocols and coding schemes such as Morse code or collaboration among the business partners, the advances would never have come about. We owe a debt of thanks to all those who persevered to bring about that revolution, and to show us the way to make our own revolutions.

Surge and Surf

If new communications technologies and stock market bubbles alike have appeared before, then why are we surprised by their occurrence in our own lifetime? Perhaps we ignore history's lessons because we lack an understanding of the repeating patterns that drive technological development.

Academic Carlota Perez uses a "surge" model to explain the long-term cycles of technological revolution.[2] Her model is derived from a range of technologies, from steam to computing, and defines two major phases in each wave of technological development. The first phase is called the "installation period," and encompasses the emergence of a new technolo-

The Life and Times of a Technology: Reoccurring phases of each great surge

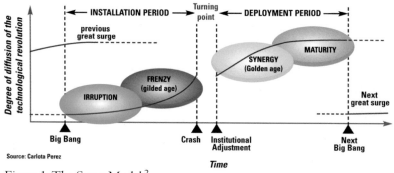

Source: Carlota Perez

Figure 1: The Surge Model[3]

gy and the frenzy of activity that accompanies it. The second phase is the "deployment period," where players use the technology in real situations and tame it, making it easier to use and more reliable.

Perez calls the growth part of this phase "synergy," but also dubs it the "golden age," in contrast to the "gilded age" of the earlier frenzy. It's a neat distinction: gilding applies a thin layer of gold to make an object appear solid gold. The deployment period tails off into "maturity," during which time the next new technology wave is building.

Microsoft's Bill Gates is reported to have said "These are the good old days" – though Google tells me Carly Simon got there first in her song *Anticipation*. According to Perez's model, the dull period when a technology delivers what it was billed to do, and creates benefits for those who invest in it, are the years of gold. I'd suggest the attributes of the golden age – the architecture of a technology's synergy – are its standards. It's standardization that makes technologies usable, understandable, predictable, secure and *spreadable*.

But it's not all about technology. (Is it ever?) Perez's self-coined term for her field of inquiry is "techno-economic paradigm shifts." That means the long waves she is describing are composed of technology and economics acting together. It's not about markets reacting to technology, but the two forces combining and playing out in the market.

Technologies Change: Standards Persist

Every cycle has its golden age, and every golden age demands its standards. Standards are the defining glue of each period of synergy. We should not therefore be surprised that while technologies may come and go, standards communities persist. These communities carry skills, practices and experiences across the generations, ensuring each viable technology reaches its period of promised delivery rather than falling to earth like a failed firework. You can see the longevity of standards communities underpinning successive waves of technologies in the persistence of bodies like ISO and ANSI – and, of course, ACORD. I've seen Perez's wave function repeat many times over the period of ACORD's existence as new technologies break on the business shore. A good proportion of the players shaken out in the aftermath of any "frenzy" are the people who fail to make the obvious, high-leverage investments in the belief only "big companies" can afford them. But if you have a data-reliant business (and show me someone who doesn't), then ignoring standards is like turning up at a war without a weapon. No, it's worse than that: it's like showing up without any pants. Not only can it be embarrassing, it can be detrimental to your success. Just look at the securities and banking industries. The power and growth created by their successful implementation of standards is now challenging insurance in a converging financial services organization.

"Standards are the defining glue."

New technologies need taming, productizing and mainstreaming in every wave. While the specifics of a technology will necessarily differ from its predecessor, many of the principles that promote its diffusion will be common with its predecessor. So too will its users. This is why ACORD standards continue to evolve through successive waves of business technology, from EDI through XML and beyond. Making technology deliver on its promise is what we're about, and that goal never changes.

WiFi

The current topic of excitement in tech circles is WiFi. By the time you read this book, WiFi will have been domesticated. As I write, a frenzy of start-ups is building WiFi hotspots to deliver wireless broadband connectivity in coffee shops and airports, while Intel's Centrino chip and its imitators are building wireless connectivity into pretty much every new laptop. We can be sure WiFi will succeed because it's standards-based: its less friendly name is the 802.11 family of wireless communications standards. Manufacturers can build WiFi product and service providers and consumers can invest in transmission and reception equipment, because there's a managed standards process to ensure interoperability and service levels.

So said *Business 2.0* magazine a few years ago to demonstrate how frictional costs represented a full 1.5 percent of U.S. domestic output."[5]

Business 2.0's characterization of economic friction is interesting in its post-Bubble focus on the costs accumulating around business transactions of all kinds, whether these are in the area of physical delivery, dealing with regulators, or accommodating and compensating employees. Whether these are really "new costs" is doubtful.

During the height of the dotcom frenzy, "the frictionless economy" was a phrase deployed to hail the beneficial effects of cheap, ubiquitous and reliable connectivity on business transactions. Wherever there was a value chain, the net – like a long-promised revolution – would set us free. The costs of finding trading partners and customers, finding out about their needs, delivering service and product to them, and taking their money – all would be lubricated by the new oil that appeared to seep out of the web (and no part of which, of course, was derived from snakes).

The friction so many dotcom startups and corporate initiatives of the Bubble years aimed to eradicate had been labeled and described as early as 1937 by economist Ronald Coase – work that won him the Nobel Prize. ACORD's 2003 Conference keynote speaker Larry Downes rediscovered Coase's theory of "transaction costs" and re-presented them for the net generation in his highly influential book *Unleashing the Killer App: Digital Strategies for Market Dominance*. Visiting Coase's work again in *The Strategy Machine: Building your business one idea at a time*, [6] Downes notes other economists estimate transaction costs account for up to 45 percent of total economic activity – or $4.5 *trillion* annually in the US alone.

Classic Economic Theory Of Transaction Costs (Coase, 1937)

Transaction Types:
- **Search:** finding each other
- **Information:** learning about each other
- **Bargaining:** setting our terms
- **Decision:** evaluating terms
- **Policing:** ensuring terms
- **Enforcement:** seeking remedies

Downes also outlines how each type of transaction cost can be reduced or removed by the use of information technology. For five of the six types of transaction costs, data standards are explicitly or implicitly the enabler of each cost's reduction or removal. (The remaining type, "search costs," is attacked by connectivity itself.)

Clearly, the concept of "economic friction" is a compelling metaphor. We can all point to areas of "stickiness" in business, and many would argue the job of strategists is to detect and correct such areas as they find, so business may run more smoothly. At ACORD we believe the responsibility to target unnecessary stickiness extends beyond the boundaries of individual organizations to the industry as a whole. By attacking waste, delay and constraint in the business network, we can expand our business opportunities. *Business 2.0*'s piece shows how the concept of friction can be applied to all kinds of barriers to trade, as well as the classical Coase transaction types, though no doubt the kinds of costs described in the article could be assigned to one or more of the categories in Coase's model.

> "Clearly, the concept of "economic friction" is a compelling metaphor."

But notice how I specify "*unnecessary* stickiness" as a target for standards. This is an important qualification, because some friction is good for us. I believe the "frictionless economy" mantra is responsible for some sloppy thinking in the realm of business-to-business transactions. Attack friction indiscriminately, and you risk throwing the baby out with the bath water. The fact is, some things just have to stick if any value is to be created.

> ""Unnecessary stickiness" is a target for standards."

Friction may be an element in a zero-sum game. Some level of friction may be natural in any economy, but the bearers of the associated costs can change. So, for example, computers (and especially networked computers) allow us to improve our productivity. But their existence causes new areas of cost. It's expensive to acquire and support systems, expensive to hire and train system developers, and even more expensive to retire systems once they no longer faithfully serve the needs of the business.

I doubt friction can be eliminated from the business environment, but I am optimistic we can keep shifting it away from the front line and into common infrastructure. This means, for example, although we may need to invest in a customer relationship management system to provide good, up-to-date information for customer service agents, we will improve the speed, accuracy and quality of the organization's customer interactions. Since our customer interactions are high on our list of values, on a holistic assessment we will profit from the change, even though we will not have zeroed the total business costs of knowing our customers.

Furthermore, I believe there are classes of friction that are not just inevitable in business, but are positively vital to its healthy functioning. These are so important I use the term *traction* to isolate and highlight them.

Where Business Grips

We use "traction" to describe a situation where we need to haul some weight: where we need to apply some temporary stickiness to make some object progress. Traction is similar to leverage. We use the force of traction to get more work done than we would otherwise accomplish. Traction is friction at our service.

Friction comes in handy in all kinds of places. It's something you want on your tires, that's for sure. And without it, physics tells us, we'd be in constant motion. A little friction keeps us sane, and safe.

In our business world, the everyday friction that makes life possible translates into permanent identities and relationships. For example, having a job is a little piece of friction tying a person to a set of responsibilities. A job makes the person and her services visible in the market. Another example would be the relationship between an agent and a carrier. These two parties agree to bind to each other around a set of common expectations about the kinds of transactions they will do with each other, the benefits enjoyed by each party, and each party's responsibilities to the other. This type of friction brings to mind the physical episode of friction with which it equates in simple markets: the handshake.

"Traction is friction at our service."

Once you have established points of useful friction, you can use them to gain traction. Returning to the example of the job, once we have a person charged with a set of responsibilities, we can motivate and reward him to achieve extraordinary feats. So much of business leadership, and training around business leadership, is aimed precisely at gaining this kind of traction. And when we turn to the area of useful friction known as relationships, we find another powerful source of potential traction. This is where the handshake strengthens into a powerful, sustained grip. The insurance industry is powered by the traction engines of its key relationships. To put it at its simplest, the players in this industry need each other. It's the only way value is generated. Customers can buy generic products from undifferentiated suppliers, but not all of them do so, or ever will. A significant proportion will always want personal service. Many will want to consider their cover, investments and general financial ambitions as a single topic with an informed and empathetic advisor. This is traction in action. Who are we to say these people should be forced to hunt for their own solutions? The fact is, when you "disintermediate" certain kinds of service, you destroy markets.

Removing unnecessary friction and promoting vital traction is the stuff of our day-to-day activities at ACORD. The standards resulting from our work are the embodiment of this ideal.

ACORD isn't a technology organization, but a *business effectiveness* organization. We exist to improve the way things get done in our industry. ACORD standards vaporize the areas of unnecessary friction that otherwise exist within organizations and between trading partners. Our standards destroy uncertainty about the meaning, format and order of the key elements in our business discourse. But they do not attack the people, organizations and principles that convey those elements. We clear away the clutter, so you can get down to business and the strategies involved.

The Rules Of Traction

- If too much sticks, then nothing gets done. But if nothing sticks, then nothing gets done.
- Replace frontline friction with infrastructure. But don't expect to zero your overall costs.
- Intermediaries add value. Those who don't will wither, with or without the help of technology.
- Intermediaries enable trading parties to reflect on their goals and state them objectively, in pursuit of win-win outcomes.
- Useful friction is a source of traction. Traction has a multiplier effect on business capability.
- Every business is a people business. Use standards to clear the paths between people, to cement their relationships, and to empower their interactions.

3

Lingua Franca

Business works through shared language

ACORD's job is to develop and promote business information standards for the insurance industry. I believe standards form the single most valuable, powerful and far-reaching asset a business can acquire in today's competitive climate and it's only recently that companies have begun to look at data as a key corporate asset. But I'm aware not everybody thinks the way we do. In this chapter, I look at the myths that have built up around standards, and where these myths come from. You've probably heard some other myths too, and if they differ from the ones I've described, do share them with me.

After I've dealt with the myths, I define exactly what I mean by standards. I look at the three different types of standards – evolutionary, revolutionary and managed standards – as well as the related topics of "proprietary standards" and regulations.

Finally, I briefly discuss why standards enlarge and enrich trading communities of all types as we all seek a "Lingua Franca" through which to transact.

Why have these myths grown around standards? And why have they persisted in the face of mounting evidence of the immense business value of standards?

The Myth Machine

Ten Myths Of Standards

1. Standards are a technology issue.
2. Standards hinder business by spreading uniformity.
3. Standards are obscure.
4. Standards are an excuse for suppliers to sell upgrades.
5. Standards stifle innovation and competitiveness.
6. Standards are bureaucratic.
7. Standards do not fix business problems.
8. Standards play no part in the success of any industry.
9. Standards always change, so why invest.
10. Standards setting is a time consuming and expensive process

I guess if you're used to traveling in a fog, and believe that fog is the natural state of the environment, then you're bound to embrace ideas that don't stand up to harsh scrutiny. These myths are part of the fog of IT, and a surprisingly respectable part of the fog. But they're irrational beliefs, like mariners' tales of serpents and monsters. These myths are stories told by people about a destination they have never visited. You'd be better off taking your cues from people who've actually deployed standards: people who live by the beacons, not the fog.

The first five of these myths share the idea standards are a vehicle for other people to impose their will where it doesn't belong. Whether it's a faceless public body needlessly trying to regularize the way businesses operate, or a shadowy cabal of technologists attempting to force-fit their view of the world on to business decision-makers, each of these myths features a hidden enemy who challenges the business's liberty.

Only an extreme libertarian would reject a tool, concept or method simply because it originated from outside his own locality, without examining its merits or investigating the outcomes achieved by other users. Yet when we knowingly ascribe the "not-invented-here syndrome" to individuals, teams or organizations we are acknowledging such rigidity is an ever-present threat to rational decision-making.

When you're in a fog, it can be easy to imagine the shadows are full of threats. Turn the lights on, and these myths are rapidly exposed as knee-jerk objections to products that originate outside the organization. It's then much easier to evaluate standards on a rational basis, looking at what they can do for your business, rather than assuming their very existence challenges your right to exist.

Some myths ramp up the suspicion level to suggest standards are intended to profit anyone other than the organization that uses them. Fear of loss is operating here. People who subscribe to these myths believe someone, somehow is going to rip them off, using the banner of "standards" as a cover.

"Fear of loss is operating here."

Yet all users of standards and objective observers report adopters of standards enjoy enhanced business success as a result of their adoption. The users profit, not the suppliers. The standards community provides a service users deploy to leverage their own businesses.

These myths are potent, and difficult to slay. But they all descend from one very simple mistake. These negative impressions of standards apply to *proprietary* standards, not genuine standards. And as we'll see, "proprietary standards" aren't standards at all.

The Three Types of Standards

There are three types of genuine standards, and then there are proprietary standards. In this section, I want to clarify what the different genuine types are. The model presented here is a novel one. It is a three-part model of standards, in which managed standards (such as ACORD's) synthesize and transcend the best features of evolutionary and revolutionary standards.

Evolutionary Standards

These standards could also be called *conciliatory.* They attempt to rationalize systems already in use, where definitions are in dispute.

A key example is the "Imperial" system of weights and measures, which is a set of standards rationalized by the monarchs of England, and latterly by the British government.

The imperial system has tried at various times to circumscribe or abolish differences of definition in different domains. For example, a fathom was six feet when used aboard a man o' war, but five and one half feet on a merchant ship, and five feet on fishing vessels and other smaller craft.[7] Pollution between different domains also caused problems: for example, the pound sterling (used to denominate money) derived from the pound weight of silver, but there were several different kinds of pound weights. So-called Troy pounds (introduced into England in 1414) were eventually standardized for the currency, but in the mid sixteenth century there were still several types of "merchant's pounds."[8]

Such evolutionary systems derive ultimately from human measures. The fathom, for example, is related to a man's height; the origin of the foot is obvious (as is its variable size throughout Europe in former times). Other measures rely on how much work a human can do (a furlong, for example, is a "farrow long," or the distance a man can push a plow before tiring), or how far he can walk in a day.

It's interesting to note the earliest attempts at "scientific management" explicitly reverse this reasoning. The focus of management rationalizers like Frederick Winslow Taylor was to fit tools to work, thereby finding the optimal measure for a set task.

The final attribute of evolutionary systems worth noting is their reliance on appointed people for their definition and enforcement. In the case of these systems, they really are "ruled." The authorities can be kings, as in the case of the English system, or priests, in the case of earlier systems of weights and measures, such as those of the Babylonians.

The Importance Of The Horse's Ass

The US standard railroad gauge (distance between the rails) is 4 feet, 8.5 inches. That's an exceedingly odd number. Why was this gauge used? Because that's the way they built them in England, and English expatriates built the US Railroads.

Why did the English build them like that? Because the first rail lines were built by the same people who built the pre-railroad tramways, and that's the gauge they used.

Why did "they" use that gauge then? Because the people who built the tramways used the same jigs and tools they used for building wagons, which used that wheel spacing.

Okay! Why did the wagons have that particular odd wheel spacing? Well, if they tried to use any other spacing, the wagon wheels would break on some of the old, long distance roads in England, because that's the spacing of the wheel ruts.

So who built those old rutted roads? Imperial Rome built the first long distance roads in Europe (and England) for their legions. The roads have been used ever since. And the ruts in the roads? Roman war chariots formed the initial ruts, which everyone else had to match for fear of destroying their wagon wheels. Since the chariots were made for Imperial Rome, they were all alike in the matter of wheel spacing.

The United States standard railroad gauge of 4 feet, 8.5 inches is derived from the original specifications for an Imperial Roman war chariot. And bureaucracies live forever. So the next time you are handed a specification and wonder what horse's ass came up with it, you may be exactly right, because the Imperial Roman war chariots were made just wide enough to accommodate the back ends of two war horses.

Now the twist to the story... When you see a Space Shuttle sitting on its launch pad, there are two big booster rockets attached to the sides of the main fuel tank. These are solid rocket boosters, or SRBs. The SRBs are made by Thiokol at their factory at Utah. The engineers who designed the SRBs would have preferred to make them a bit fatter, but the SRBs had to be shipped by train from the factory to the launch site. The railroad line from the factory happens to run through a tunnel in the mountains. The SRBs had to fit through that tunnel. The tunnel is slightly wider than the railroad track, and the railroad track, as you now know, is about as wide as two horses' behinds. So, a major Space Shuttle design feature of what is arguably the world's most advanced transportation system was determined over two thousand years ago by the width of a horse's ass....

And you thought being a horse's ass wasn't important?

Revolutionary Standards

These standards could also be called *disruptive*. They attempt to create new systems based on reason alone, which will be applicable universally. A key example is the metric system, which was created as a conscious revolutionary act in France. The system as laid out by its inventors was ruthlessly rational. The metric system is seen as largely benign throughout most of the world, although it is regarded with suspicion in the US, which nevertheless introduced the world's first decimal currency.[9] The metric system divorces standards from human models both in the unit measures and their multiples.

Parts of the French Revolutionary system failed as spectacularly as the meter *et al* succeeded. The Revolutionary calendar of ten months, and ten-day weeks, was barely observed before being dropped. Its design was meant explicitly to remove the taint of religion from the calendar: a good example of how standardization can be misused for political or ideological ends.

Metric time, at the level of granularity above the second, did not catch on either. It seems that systems of standards only enjoy support when they can be readily associated with human features, traits or habits. The twelve hours of daytime seem to fit the way we want to regard time, as does the sixty-minute hour. We could argue that the acceptability of the meter is based on its rough equivalence to a yard, which is itself based on the length of a man's arm, and not on the rigor of the meter's modern scientific definition. It is noticeable that metric users prefer the centimeter for small-scale measurements rather than the millimeter, which rationality demands we use; the centimeter is in the scale of the human finger, as is the inch.

Where evolutionary standards attempt to reconcile diversity or supersede it with new definitions for traditional quantities, revolutionary standards attempt to suppress difference. They also attempt to erase any linkage with banned regimes. They represent the extreme of social engineering. A contemporary example is the euro currency, a currency which buries the historical baggage of its constituent members, but which has scaled itself to the world's most accepted medium of exchange, the US dollar.

Managed Standards

These standards could also be called *consensual.* These systems of standards attempt to combine the best of the evolutionary and revolutionary approaches. The negotiation between the two extremes is itself governed through reference to a known user group. Whereas evolutionary systems attempt to recognize differences between domains and encourage tolerance (and conversion) across domains, managed systems look to define areas of commonality and promote the use of common elements amongst different domains. And whereas revolutionary systems attempt to impose pure reason on human affairs, managed systems make use of scientific insight as a source of guidance alongside input from other stakeholders.

A key example is Organization for Standarization (ISO). ISO is a dedicatedly global body, which is the first clue to its enduring success. Unlike the English, who dominated world trade with their "imperial" measures and ambitions, or the French, who tried to convert Europe to rationalism through wars and laws, ISO represents a multi-national mission to discover mechanisms that will have the greatest usability, acceptability and reliability amongst its broad user base.

In this kind of system, decision-making is vested neither in kings nor scientists (whether "pure" or "political") but in the users themselves. That is, those who benefit from the standards organize themselves to create, promote and deploy the standards.

This is the realm of "standards bodies": corporate beings summoned into existence to serve populations of those who would trade with each other, whether in goods, coin or ideas. Such bodies aim to be inclusive, and to facilitate transferability and repeatability via standards.

I'm proud to list ACORD as a leading example of a managed standards body.

Proprietary Standards

The three types of standards I've described cover the essential types of standards that exist in all areas of human endeavor. It may look like there's a missing type: that of proprietary standards. But it's right we don't include these. That's because "proprietary standards" aren't standards at all.

"Proprietary" means that something is held in private ownership. It also has the extended meaning of restriction. Proprietary goods and services are protected by licenses, trademarks and other forms of control. Also, the primary beneficiary of proprietary standards is the "owner" of those standards, not those that use them.

Now a *standard* is a measure by which things are judged to conform. Using standards implies comparison of foreign objects to a set model. The concept of a standard breaks down in a sterile environment. If there's no introduction of external matter into a situation, then there's no need for standards. And if a standard cannot be used to judge an external object, then it's not a standard.

It irks me that we have to support "open standards" when *all* true standards are open. You don't have to buy a license to use the dollar, or pay a royalty every time you use a tape measure. But you do pay, through your taxes, for the maintenance of such standards. That's because these standards are community benefits. They provide the essential lubrication of business. They form a common benefit with a common cost.

So what then is a "closed standard"? It must be the same animal as a proprietary standard: no standard at all.

Proprietary protocols, models, techniques, phrases, logos and so on exist to extract economic benefit from intellectual property. And there's nothing wrong with that. Without property mechanisms such as trademarks and patents, inventors and investors could not safeguard their interests and innovation would be stifled. But these mechanisms create areas of monopoly, and monopolies cannot be allowed to invade all areas of business — par-

TOLL BOOTH

ticularly not those that concern the interaction of businesses with each other, and with their customers. If an organization attempts to apply a proprietary "standard" to a communications market, then there may be constitutional issues of free speech to deal with, let alone anti-monopolies legislation. But at the practical level, proprietary "standards" for interactions are simply doomed to extinction by simple math — and simple opportunism.

Telecom Standards

Look at it this way. Users of GSM (Global System for Mobile communications) cell phones have long had the ability to send each other text messages, using the Short Message Service (SMS) facility built into GSM phones. Phone users in Europe and Asia send billions of these messages every year, and US users are fast catching up. The ability to send and receive 160-character plain text messages was built into GSM as a technical nice-to-have, but without any specific business plan. (An example of the network technocrats not staying close to the ground, but getting their head.) SMS was rarely used until carriers began to allow messages to cross from one network to another, when the market boomed. It became possible to send messages to any cell phone user without having to think about whether or not they would receive the message.

The SMS system was part of an open standard, GSM. But the network restrictions applied by the carriers had made each implementation of the standard a proprietary mechanism. Furthermore, few users within each network regarded the domain of people they wanted to contact as identical to the signed-up population of their network provider. They didn't love SMS enough to persuade their friends to switch phone companies so they could text each other. Now they love it: now that everyone's got what they already had, but couldn't use.

"People only join networks that have the potential for unlimited reach."

However you dress it up, the math of networks says people only join networks that have the potential for unlimited reach. The economic logic of networks — the corollary to this simple math — is people won't join a limited network.

Open Standards

Standards work in exactly the same way. Since standards are about conformance and exchange, they imply the coexistence of networks. There's no point learning to read and write, for example, if you have no access to some kind of delivery technology – unless you're content to commune with the dead and leave your thoughts to posterity. Similarly, there's no point in learning to read and write a language that has closed its doors to change, and that seeks to exploit its users for financial gain.

At this point we have to be clear that standards – open standards, if you want to hammer home the point – don't come for free. Standards have to be built, agreed to, maintained and promoted. These processes cost money. But there is no reason why they should be a source of profit to anyone other than their users.

I'd like to propose a tidying up of our discourse around this subject. Let's agree that a standard that isn't open is no standard at all. And let's agree that what's proprietary are the uses people make of standards, and the data they store and transact using those standards. Then we'll have a clearer shared understanding of where the boundaries between private and common ownership are.

> **"Standards have to be built, agreed to, maintained and promoted."**

Regulations

Some standards are put in the form of regulations. This means they are enforced by law. In Europe, for example, it is illegal to sell fruit and vegetables using any measure other than kilograms and grams. British market traders who proudly offer pounds of apples are sometimes prosecuted.[10] The reason for making and enforcing such rules is consumer protection. If competing systems of measurement are allowed to co-exist, then there is (the argument goes) scope for traders to abuse the resulting confusion.

Although regulations embody standards, regulations are not a *distinct* type of standards. Any type of standard, whether it is evolutionary, revolutionary or managed, can be given the power of law. The metric system's legality in European weights and measures is an example of a revolutionary standard being used to create a regulation. The dollar's status as the sole currency of the US is a similar example.

Managed standards can become regulations too. Despite being created by and for groups of users, managed standards can be given the force of law. Their benefits can, if you will, be forced upon their users. The healthcare data standard HL7, for example, is mandated by the US government for all transactions undertaken with its agencies. If you don't comply, you can find yourself facing a fine.

Talking and Trading

Lingua Franca: a beautiful phrase meaning a language that serves as a common medium between different spoken languages. *Lingua Franca* actually means "the Frankish tongue." This mongrel language was originally used in the eastern Mediterranean region, and was made up of bits of Italian, French, Greek, Arabic and Spanish. Today, we're left with a *Latin* phrase that appears to mean *French*, and which is often used to describe the world-class communications standard of *English*… which is actually *American*.

The original users of "the Frankish tongue" were clearly traders: business people transacting goods and services in one of the old world's greatest crossing areas. They adopted words from each other's languages to ensure they could trade effectively – building, if you will, a common language from the most easily understood and most stable common words. Today's "business English" directly threatens other languages by injecting terms like "software" and "web" into French and German. Our shrinking world communicates largely through a shifting but recognizable set of words held in common and hence concepts. Our shared words underpin shared models of the world.

> **"Our shared words underpin shared models of the world."**

Any *Lingua Franca* is a de facto standard: one generated by the population that uses it. De facto standards are often baroque in nature, exhibiting charming quirks that could not have come from any committee. The word "googol," for example, refers to the number represented by a one with 100 zeros after it. The web's leading search engine Google is named in honor of this suitably awesome number. The word's original devisor, having run out of names modeled on *billion* and *trillion*, and presumably unwilling to annex the slang word *bazillion*, based "googol" on the sounds that his young child was making at the time.

Spoken language is full of attractively peculiar derivations. But planned standards, or de jure standards, are more rationally based. Rational standards aim to model some domain in as neutral a fashion as possible, so that parties with an interest in that domain can communicate meaningfully with each other. Such standards are, first and foremost, about clarity of definition. If we regard computers and networks as extensions of human communications systems, then rational standards also have a prime role to play in helping our automated systems to collaborate with each other in pursuit of our shared business goals. This is where standards such as ACORD's come in to play. The standardization of the insurance industry's commercial tongues can contribute massively to greater commerce, and to greater innovation.

> "Standards are, first and foremost, about clarity of definition."

Coins

The earliest practical de jure standards are metal coins. A coinage is a form of stable, printed token which guarantees to store and transmit value amongst people who recognize the ultimate authority and credibility of the imagery and messages shown on the coin. Coins allow us to transact with each other using a neutral, rationally based and - crucially - constrained set of tokens. We no longer have to argue that one man's sheep is worth another man's firewood: both parties can agree on a sum of money as a mediating mechanism, knowing they can convert that sum into other goods or services at other times. All parties using the coinage know it is stable: it will not suddenly be changed, devalued or recalibrated. Before long, markets, professions and dynasties are founded on the uses and movements of money alone, divorced from any tangible real-world exchange item.

Coins still have the power to create strong communities of interest. The Euro is history's greatest example of a de jure standard intended to inculcate commercial (and ideological) commonality amongst a set of hitherto diverse groups. The EU's intention with the introduction of the Euro is to improve the economic standing of the trading block by easing cross-border transactions and creating a world currency to rival the dollar. Cooperation and collaboration across Europe's internal borders, long encouraged by market-focused reforms, have been finally underscored by the withdrawal of national currencies. It is as though the EU has mandated a kind of Esperanto, and ordered the destruction of individual languages and de facto "Frankish tongues" alike.

Clearly, standards that are guided and nurtured by bodies with long-term aims can produce striking market effects. The committee room is not always the enemy of the trading floor. Common coins allow us to trade: common terms allow us to communicate: common world models allow us to grow together.

Standards and Standard-bearers

Beware of any proposed business information standard whose chief claim to fame is "it's in XML." That's like saying a book must be good because it's written with words.

XML is a great meta-language for describing standards and transporting documents written in those standards, but it's no substitute for the standards themselves.

As technology stands today, XML is the primary champion of the bold idea that data sets should be closely coupled with the data models that give them meaning. Other technologies may take over this role in the future. What will endure are those sound data models that are expressed through XML.

Think of it this way. The information you need to exchange with other parties is content. You pack content in cans that are labeled according to agreements in your industry, so anyone involved knows exactly what to do with any can. XML is a way of manufacturing cans and gluing labels to them. Clearly, it's the label that's important to the business in the long run.

Ring-pull cans, self-cooking cans, square cans — who knows what improvements in storage and transmission technologies the future will bring us. Yet being able to read those labels is going to be the enduring investment — and the enduring rationale for any system that surrounds them.

4

Why IT Projects Fail

How standards make winners

This chapter examines why information systems projects tend to go wrong, and how standards can ensure they go right. Wise project managers will recognize many of the messages here, and will also know there is plenty more to be said on delivering IT successfully into the enterprise. I've tried to focus on the crucial role of standards, and to relate the benefits of standards to the dominant characteristics of projects. I hope the result proves the risk-reducing and quality-enhancing effect of standards in a way that chimes with the experience of our successful adopters throughout the industry and around the world.

There's no shortage of advice on why projects fail. Business people, engineers, military planners – they've been watching projects crash and burn for generations. Their observations have taught them a lot. Successful projects – the ones we applaud, and then rapidly take for granted as they deliver their promised benefits into the stream of everyday business – owe much of their success to the learning we derive from past failures. As a problem-solving species, we advance by refinement of prior approaches as much as by sudden mental breakthroughs. We're experimenters, observers and learners.

In the case of ACORD standards, current developments in IT dictate XML as the preferred medium for our standards. XML is the nearest we have to a universal carrier or substrate for standards in the current era. XML is supported by all the major platform providers, is compatible with every popular development environment, and is increasingly at the heart of commercial packaged software solutions. XML gives us a short cut to the widest possible set of compatible technologies.

It follows that simply by adopting a reputable standard at the heart of your project, your technology risks are diluted.

Under-resourced

We didn't have the money, people or time we needed to pull in a winner. The nature of standards production also ensures the metrics around their implementation are well known within their community of users. Organizations that have adopted a standard can tell you how their use changed the loading pattern of their project, helping you to determine when and where you need to apply resource.

Mistimed

We did everything right, but the environment changed around us: the organization merged with another one, "the business" changed priorities on us, or a competitor stole a march on us. We ended up working a "wrong problem!"

Standards that address communication amongst parties, as ACORD's do, incorporate a degree of insulation against the misreading of business evolution. They also provide hedging of a project's investment in the case where it is put on ice or set to compete with a rival in, say, a company merger.

The remaining five factors are comic. They refer to in-project failings that are so well known we can hardly imagine a good excuse for their recurrence.

No change management

We had no system for accepting, documenting and progressing changes to the project's requirements. Either we kidded ourselves nothing would change, or we couldn't be bothered.

Bad estimating

We didn't really define in detail the goals and scope of the project. We put the wrong time and cost estimates on the project's tasks. Both bad estimations might be because we lacked the necessary experience, or because we felt under pressure to produce the "right" project plan rather than an achievable one with realistic expectations.

Team dynamics

We didn't get along with each other. And we didn't try to fix broken relationships, power struggles, or differences of opinion. The potential creativity of the project's people never gelled into a performing team.

Poor communications

We didn't tell our users or our sponsors what we were doing. We didn't talk amongst ourselves. We didn't write anything down.

Lack of user involvement

We knew better than to include the target user group of the project. They'd have only asked for changes, or questioned the rationale of the project.

Loss of organizational sponsorship

There was no internal business owner or driver for the project, therefore the organization gave up on us. When the going got tough, the tough went shopping.

Fighting Fail Factors

Nowhere in our list of fail factors is the statement: "Standards let us down." That would be like a business pointing to the accounting rules as a reason for missing its numbers, or a losing race car driver blaming the laws of mechanics.

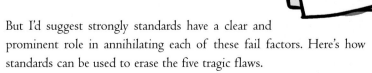

But I'd suggest strongly standards have a clear and prominent role in annihilating each of these fail factors. Here's how standards can be used to erase the five tragic flaws.

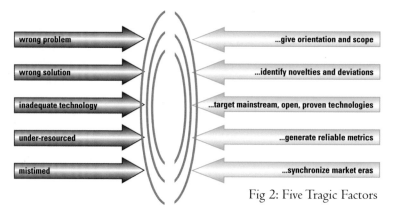

wrong problem	...give orientation and scope
wrong solution	...identify novelties and deviations
inadequate technology	...target mainstream, open, proven technologies
under-resourced	...generate reliable metrics
mistimed	...synchronize market eras

Fig 2: Five Tragic Factors

Swim in the Mainstream

Since ACORD's standards enable business partners to interoperate using a common language, it stands to reason their wide use plays a part in influencing the evolutionary direction of the industry. That's right: by using ACORD standards, you are swimming in the mainstream of the industry. You're picking up the scent your peers and competitors have sensed, and bottled. Ideally, you should be playing a part in the formulation of those standards, since the creativity and expertise of your organization is an important factor in the development of the industry. But even if you choose to stay out of the standards-setting activity, you still benefit from the slipstream effect standards create. The energy of standards contributes to the drive mechanism of the industry. If you're on board, you're less likely to be left behind.

Where events wrong-foot your projects in a manner entirely separate from the trajectory of the industry as a whole, your use of standards can mark a significant protection of the organization's investment to date. If your project is temporarily shelved, or joined with another project, its achievements to date will be legible, rational and usable when the time comes to reactivate it. If the project becomes part of a project not using standards, you can bet standards will carry the day. The productivity and provability benefits of standards – let alone their other virtues – will infect any new host project. From the point of view of the initiating project, its work lives on. This isn't a matter of salvaging what we can from a failed project, or painting a rosy picture of a crash, but a genuine recognition of the lasting benefit standards bring to the business ventures that embrace them. Standards are a capped investment: you always get your principle back, even if the market fails.

What about the five comic failings? Here's a reminder of those fail factors:
No change management
- Bad estimating
- Team dynamics
- Poor communications
- Lack of user involvement
- Loss of organizational sponsorship

We looked at "bad estimating" in the context of standards' role in the removal of resourcing errors. That role is a good example of how standards act as a vehicle of communication — in this case, communication of labor and duration requirements. Standards embody a common vocabulary for the domain they address, so they can act as a dictionary for all kinds of communications purposes. Change management systems, for example, can be built around entities or groups of entities in a standard model, with related project products hanging from the structure. Standards can be used to allocate or influence team roles and relationships, thereby removing potential areas of duplication or misunderstanding.

How Standards Shape the "Project Box"

Experienced project managers will be familiar with the following model or some variant of it. I call this model "the project box." It's the fundamental business shape of every project that has ever been, and ever will be, carried out.

Organizations attempt to optimize the shape of the box against the four dimensions of cost, function, quality and time. (By the way, I don't mean to imply any priority in this list: it's simply alphabetical.) Changing a value on any one of the dimensions affects the others. For example, if we shrink the time available for a project, then these are some of the revised project shapes that may result:

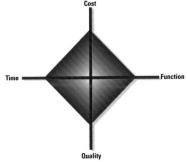

Fig 3: The Classic Project Box

In the first example, higher costs are applied to meet the time constraint without degrading any of the other dimensions. In the second example, quality is sacrificed to time, with cost and function maintained. In the third example, both the functional scope and the quality of the project are diminished to cater for the compressed timeline.

Fig 4: Deformations

Project managers know when a target on one of the project's dimensions is revised, "something's got to give." In many organizations, project costs are supposedly capped and non-negotiable; but we know from the proportion of over-budget projects in every walk of life this rule is most often honored in the breach. Nevertheless, cost containment is usually the chief priority when any of a project's other boundaries are revised. Inevitably, quality and functional coverage suffer, and projects are delivered late.

A Higher Probability of Success

How can standards help to shape and insure healthy project boxes — projects that fully meet their goals on each dimension, and which are robust in the face of changing targets?

First, standards help project teams to establish initial project boxes with higher probability of viability than those built without the use of standards. Since standards embody the combined experience and best advice of professionals working in the same domain as yourself, they give you a massive head start in determining a realistic shape for your project. Standards provide a candidate subject scope for the project, which you can trim to your own needs. This scope can be used in turn to control the population of your functional specification. Above all, the knowledge capital contained within standards guarantees your ability to hit the quality mark.

Second, standards provide a tailored set of metrics against which a project box can be calibrated. They allow you to measure degrees of completion for various work packages, and to measure deviation from plan when one or other of the project's dimensions is impacted. In other words, standards provide a global management tool to control the deformation and reformation of the project box when its shape is challenged by changing targets, as well as affording a means of understanding and reporting progress during normal times.

Imagine your standards set as a net stretched between the four poles of the project box. It is flexible, yet it provides an evenly distributed unifying force amongst the four dimensions that bound the project. The use of standards nullifies the otherwise overwhelming effect a change in, say, time horizon can have on a project. Without standards, the effect of a change in delivery target will have an unpredictable effect on the other dimensions. The degree to which each of the related dimensions suffers will depend largely on the taste of the project manager, or luck. So, if "quality" has always been a vague term in the team's environment, the quality target will be quietly lost to the revised delivery challenge.

"Standards provide a global management tool."

When standards are in place, the multiplex relationship that applies amongst the boundaries of the project box is given tangible, legible form. If you cut a project's timeline, areas of functionality determined by the reference standards will begin to flash warning lights. The team will rapidly recognize how completion, cost or quality of the functional scope will be affected — and can work with these effects at a micro level. Instead of accepting the vague feeling "something's got to give," the team can evaluate a range of scenarios to fit the new requirements. So, for example, the team might work up a revised project plan in which 25 percent of a project's functionality is removed to allow a ten percent reduction in timeline. Still using the standards as reference, the team can then use this scenario as the topic for a business discussion. Is the 25 percent lost functionality truly marginal? Or is it included in the business benefits the shortened project is meant to achieve?

The enterprise can then rule on the implementation effects of its decision. The organization may say: We accept we'll lose 25 percent of the functionality of this project, but if we don't hit our revised target we'll miss the market opportunity. Therefore, let's work on the scenario to make sure we've bundled the right functions in the 25 percent reduction – the ones we can live without at this time. Or the organization may say: We can't sacrifice any of the functionality, but we must still hit the new date. How then can we change the resourcing of the project to make sure we achieve our new goal?

This process of measuring the impact of change and negotiating an optimal response is the stuff of good business management. The examples I've described here should resonate across all kinds of projects and industries. But I maintain this kind of practice simply is not followed in organizations that don't use standards. The absence of standards means there is no common vocabulary, model or set of practices to control the discussion. And without that mediating function, the needed conversations do not occur.

Let Standards Be Your Compass

If you don't have a compass, then you're not going to start arguing about whether you should head north, south, east or west. The concept just won't enter your head. Let standards be your compass, your guidebook, and your odometer. You'll wonder how you ever managed to make a project box withstand the buffeting of delivery in a typically harsh and unpredictable business climate. The truth is, without standards, everything you accomplish is makeshift. So, when your project box comes under pressure:

• Use standards to demarcate the areas of impact
• Use standards to drive precise re-estimation of the impact of change
• Use standards to dialog the business's detailed response to the needed change

Having standards in place ensures once the project box begins to feel the pressure of change, it adapts rather than buckling. It's like having your production process shot through with an immensely strong, flexible fiber that "remembers" its original shape. Another way to put it: add standards to the mix of your business, and you bake in integrity.

5

Innovation

Using standards to take the business to the next level

Can standards make your organization smarter? Or are they just about making your mainline processes slicker?

Standards have a key role in providing business efficiency, and ACORD's roots are firmly in the reduction of waste, duplication and delay. In fact, ROI cases for standards can readily be written for organizations on the basis of internal process improvement alone.

But this is just the beginning of the story. Standards also provide a foundation on which the organization can build new capabilities, products and markets. They open up the pathway to commercial creativity on a grand scale.

The development and adoption of standards within an industry proceed hand-in-hand with the growth of an industry. It's almost impossible — except with hindsight — to separate the two phenomena. Does market growth encourage the formulation of standards, or is it the other way round? In reality, both statements are true. There's a virtuous relationship between both forces. Growing markets inspire standards, while the existence of standards encourages markets to grow. In this chapter we see how standards and innovation work hand-in-glove to propel markets and enhance businesses.

Standards Put Enterprises Ahead

A study[11] by the German Standards Institute (DIN) in May 2000 listed a series of economic benefits of standards. These are the highlights:

- Standards contribute more to economic growth than patents and licenses.
- Standards have a strategic significance in companies.
- Companies that participate actively in standards work have a head start on their competitors in adapting to market demands.
- Research risks and development costs are reduced for companies contributing to the standardization process.
- Businesses that are actively involved in standards work more frequently reap short- and long-term benefits with regard to costs and competitive status than those who do not participate.
- Standards are a positive stimulus for innovation.

Emerging Behavior

Standards are a natural outcome of growth. No significant area of human endeavor can grow to maturity and dominance without also developing standards. Standards form a temporal infrastructure, if you will: a path to the future.

Standards such as weights and measures evolve as trade becomes widespread and draws in a wider variety of buyers, sellers and transacted items. Rulers or revolutionaries step in to bring order to competing standards. And concerned stakeholders organize themselves to measure the development and promotion of standards for the benefit of their membership. But there's another way of looking at the development of standards, and the superiority of managed standards, and that is to approach the topic from the fashionable angle of network science, or "emergence."

I'm not going to push the loud pedal on the subject of emergence, since there are many excellent books on the subject that do a better job of explaining it. However, I would like to show a very simple model of emergence that suggests itself from my experience with systems and standards, and which can be described in terms of market evolution.

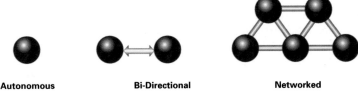

| Autonomous | Bi-Directional | Networked |

Figure 5: Evolution of Markets

Let's start with a simple market, which I'll call the autonomous state. In the past, the great majority of products, services, concepts and policies launched into markets were aimed at changing the behavior or benefits of individuals. Even where those individuals were seen in the mass, they were still addressed as autonomous parties. From the point of view of selling a product, the product was described in terms of the benefits its features provided. This is the autonomous state, where market players seek to pose and answer the question "Who am I?"

The goal in this era of the market is to change an individual's local behavior. This may include his view of himself, or his identification or allegiance with other groups or concepts. The key factor is the individual's ability to effect the desired change without any further input or agreement.

As markets become more sophisticated, products and services emerge which require bi-directional relationships. Even though behavior-changing messages are addressed to individuals, those individuals must respond by entering into relationships with another party. The nature of each bi-directional relationship introduced to the market is unique to itself. The relationship is designed to service its committed parties.

The goal of marketers in this era is to answer the individual's question: "What's in it for me?" Individuals invest in relationships, and cede a degree of autonomy. The benefits of the arrangement must be demonstrated to outweigh the inconvenience of change, and the partial loss of autonomy.

As markets adjust to bi-directional relationships and begin to take their benefits for granted, individuals begin to notice operational duplication. Factoring out common aspects of the proliferating relationships and standardizing them will bring savings to all players. Yet this truth only occurs to those outside the emerging network, or players within the network who have foresight, together with community spirit and/or an economic motive for helping to reduce the wasted effort. Despite their vision, haphazard networking continues.

Behavior in this era of the market is ruled by habit. New relationships are forged on the model of existing ones, but without reusing any of their operational machinery. It is as if every banknote is painted by hand: the resulting bills are expensive to produce and open to counterfeiting, but they are the best bills we have.

Strategists face a monumental challenge in moving beyond this era. They know how to sell individuals through benefits linked to features. They know how to sell bi-directional relationships, and have built processes to support those relationships. The market is now invested in a range of proprietary solutions, which all continue to function. No one can stop the clock of business so the underlying machinery can be consolidated into a cheaper, better common infrastructure. Now marketers want to sell solutions to this deep problem, without disrupting business or alienating buyers. How do they proceed?

Some players have attempted to resolve this problem by positioning themselves as universal resolvers of relationships, or hubs. It's as if the airlines operators all decide they're making too many flights and customers could save time and money by all being switched through Atlanta. There will be the odd frustrated traveler who has to fly from Portland, Oregon to San Francisco, California via Atlanta, but the overall benefit to the industry will overwhelm any objections with its cool logic, won't it? Well, no.

While I believe intermediaries can add significant value to markets, I don't believe mediation is the answer to every problem. Some superhighways become bottlenecks. And sometimes the solution to a traffic problem is a beltway.

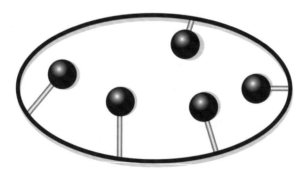

Figure 6: Standardization Simplifies Markets

Standards flip the logic of the hub solution inside out. Instead of forcing traders through a central point of coordination, we give every trader the means of communicating clearly, effectively and reliably with every other trader. We dissolve the connectivity into the business processes of the industry. It's like laying on water and power. Businesses tap into the logical ether supplied by standards, and they can do so with little conscious thought.

Standards embody and enact the truth that individuals who wish to enjoy the benefits of relationships can be part of a wider community, at lower cost, by adopting the standards than by sticking with their existing arrangements. They form an alternate reality to challenge the make-do that surrounds us. They are the practical distillation of vision.

> "Standards are an emergent property of complex networks."

I believe standards are an emergent property of complex networks. This means standards are a co-product of success. As inter-communicating communities become larger and more active, they must craft and adopt standards for their own survival and growth.

The difference between our own age and previous eras is our sophisticated modern world will not let us evolve standards over generations. It is already clear the power and reach of the Internet is challenging our traditional legislative and regulatory frameworks. Just look at the trauma the phenomenon of spam is causing government agencies around the globe. Enterprises cannot wait for governments to act on spam (assuming they even can act effectively) but must formulate their own strategies for blocking unwanted message traffic. Similarly, enterprises cannot wait for "the establishment" (for want of a better phrase) to solve its business interoperability issues. This is something we have to do for ourselves: with common cause, in concert.

Transferability

Standards enable transferability: from person to person, time to time and/or place to place. Transfer across time can also be called durability or repeatability, depending on the type of object to which the concept is applied. This is why we call currency "a store of value" as well as "a means of exchange."

The earliest standards were weights. Standard weights allow people to trade fairly, ensuring they are not cheated when they barter goods. As commerce became more important to human society, various types of currency were invented to introduce liquidity into markets. This meant traders no longer needed to negotiate about the relative and proportional values of, say, sheep versus corn. Currency allows us to transact in a common format we know can be converted into appropriate quantities of sheep, corn, or anything else.

Coins are a natural development of the weights system, since they were originally based on specific weights of precious metals. But as coins became more widespread, their practicality declined. Coins could be snipped, hollowed out or "sweated" to degrade their true value. With the passage of time, even unaltered coins lost some weight due to handling. Coins from some sources were trusted more than others. Generally speaking, the farther a coin wandered, the less trusted it was. (Some coins achieved global acceptability, such as the Spanish real: the original "piece of eight" pirates, or their parrots, were supposedly so fond of.)

Currency was further standardized through the application of industrial processes. The manufacture of coins, and the invention of edge-milling ensured uniformity and stability in every coin put into circulation. The advent of paper money also relied on industrial processes, particularly new methods of steel engraving invented by Jacob Perkins.[12]

Industrialization is itself a process of standardization. Ford's assembly line enabled the rapid production of low-cost automobiles. Later developments in industry created standard parts. We can now organize businesses according to supply chains, confident, parts from different suppliers will fit or work together in a defined fashion.

As well as the property of ensured transferability, all these species of standards show two further common attributes: authority and transparency.

Authority

Authority is the assurance a user gets that something produced according to a standard will meet his needs. Early authorities for weights and measures were often priests or other leaders of their communities. The authorities behind money were originally monarchs (sometimes annexing the authority of gods), and then governments, and now "the authorities" that regulate the financial markets. Industry has relied on several levels of authority, including those of the professions (for example, mechanical engineering tolerances), governments (for example, the granting of telecommunications licenses), monopolies, industry groupings and the market ("de facto" standards).

Transparency

Transparency is the ability of a standardized item to expose its own function without additional explanation. A dollar bill explains its function in writing, and is easily demonstrated in use. A standard weight tips a set of scales. A standard plug fits a standard socket, and the appliance works. (The connector of the keyboard on which I'm writing this text is a DIN plug, named for the standards organization whose findings opened this chapter.)

A Platform for Innovation

Platform is a term that has been co-opted by the technology industry to mean many things. It normally refers to a computer's operating system; though, as we shall see, with the rapid development of new Internet standards, platform is coming to mean the net itself. "Platform" is also used in the wider world to mean a political position; a body of ideas and interests giving a coherent voice to a common cause within the community.

I look at ACORD's role as a platform provider, combining both senses of the word and putting the emphasis on empowerment. We will use platform to mean a solid place from which players can move upward and onward in their missions. ACORD's platform contains technology elements, yes: but its primary feature is its enabling, foundational nature for business developers and deliverers.

Standards Drive Innovation

Standards and innovation are not often mentioned in the same breath — but they should be. Good standards and smart innovation go together like sound money and thriving markets. Once a community shares a common language, members can talk with each other more easily, and, crucially, develop more sophisticated ideas, organizations and processes.

ACORD has laid a solid foundation of shared standards for the insurance community. The primary role of ACORD's standards has historically been to enable data transactions. The use of standards within the insurance domain eliminates rekeying of data when information is exchanged between systems, saving both time and potential costly errors. Removing human error from system-to-system communication is an achievement, but it's only the start of ACORD's work.

> **"Eliminate rekeying of data when information is exchanged between systems."**

Once standards are in place, and being used daily by thousands of users to exchange millions of data items, the standards melt into the business systems environment. They become part of the furniture: useful, relied upon, maintained, but not especially treasured.

This is how it should be. We don't need to marvel that everyone drives on the same side of the road every time we start the car. We're more interested in where our journey will take us. It's the same with data standards. With ACORD's established standards, users can take for granted their data payloads will be delivered on target. The trusted foundation in place, we can start to look for new ways to do business, new partners to do business with, and new markets to do business in.

We're on a journey that takes in new routes, new companions, and new destinations. Standards drive innovation as sure as roads inspire discovery.

Web Services Widen Options

The good news is the Internet technology community has taken these what-if's, learned from the lessons of earlier proponents of interoperability, and produced a set of enabling tools to make all these things happen. The technology is grouped under the heading of "web services."

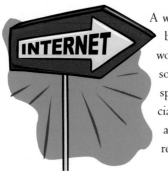

A web service is a piece of autonomous systems behavior that sits throbbing away on the network, doing a useful job for other pieces of software. Web services are a little like tireless specialists, working efficiently at their own specialties, and interacting with other specialists and generalists using simple request and response mechanisms.

The classic web service in the business context is the credit checker. A credit checker web service takes in customer identifiers and puts out credit scores. This is a function used, in various forms and for various purposes, by many thousands of organizations every day. Normally the function is provided by a third party, although some organizations, for example banks, create their own credit scores. Wrapping the credit checker service as a web service means the function can be used, over the network, by any other system. Of course, access can be restricted, charged for and so on: web services need not herald a free-for-all.

On the larger stage, the best example of a web service is Google's search engine. Other systems can now use Google's functionality just by calling its web service. The investment in performance and credibility made by Google has effectively been deployed not as a complex, hard-to-install, expensive-to-acquire product, as might have occurred in the past. Google is taking its core capability to a wide market as a service instead.

None of this would matter if the web services strategy were hard to implement. And although the list of acronyms under the web services umbrella can be daunting, the actual technologies they represent are effective, elegant, and non-proprietary. The web services standards have been created and managed through the same lightweight, open processes used to deliver the highly successful base standards of the Internet, such as HTML. They have also been supported, and driven, by the major players in the IT industry.

Web services allow us to take pieces of business functionality and offer them to other users. These users can be other systems within the organization or systems that reside somewhere else entirely. Sounds like a good way to drive those static standards off the shelf and into the arms of colleagues, partners and customers? You're right. The journey's about to get interesting.

XML & Web Services

How could we get this far in a story about standards and innovation without mentioning the adaptability of XML? The answer is XML is at the heart of web services. ACORD's move to XML as a vehicle for its standards has enlarged the appeal of the standards, allowing us to use standard

> "XML is at the heart of web services."

development toolsets and to leverage the broad-based XML skills being developed in every industry. XML also brings business meaning to the forefront of the system developer's concerns, meaning discussions between developers and business clients are rooted in business terminology, relationships and concerns from the off.

I like to describe XML in a downhome manner in terms of cans and labels. I don't do this to detract from its creators' achievements, but to stress how quickly XML has become part of the furniture. XML seems here to stay. But even if it is superseded, business standards expressed in XML will endure, and XML-based systems will migrate to the successor technology with ease. There's no undoing the openness and semantic integrity XML has brought to the world of information management.

So ACORD's XML standards ensure longevity for organizations using them. XML's place in the web standards world makes ACORD's standards first-class players in a wider world today as well. By using XML, we're making insurance functionality applicable and accessible to parties in other domains — and massively increasing the potential territory for insurance players to build and execute creative new businesses.

Integration

Enough of the build-up: Where is this journey really taking us? Let's start close to home, with the systems inside an organization. Making legacy systems talk with each other has been an expensive, time-consuming and frustrating escapade for many dedicated teams in organizations all over the world. The goal doesn't just affect long-established organizations, although its effect is easily experienced in such places. Systems integration is as big an issue for new players, because few manage to launch or sustain their businesses without using packaged software or acquiring other businesses. Mergers and acquisitions, and the use of commercial software packages, rapidly introduce diversity into the purest of startups.

Before web services, systems integration had to be achieved on an ad hoc basis. Specialists would examine the interfaces of target systems, and design bridges between them. In some cases they were able to build or acquire toolkits to save some of the effort, especially where most of the target systems had been built on only a handful of platforms. (There goes that "platform" word again. Makes you wonder why we ever allowed the little critter to have a plural.)

Some services firms grew rich on systems integration work. Even they found it hard to reuse experience from one job to the next without narrowing their focus too much. Companies emerged to offer "enterprise application integration" (EAI) toolsets, but no EAI offering could solve every problem thrown at it.

> **"Systems integrators need no longer build or debate which common data model they should use."**

Using ACORD's standards in XML, systems integrators need no longer build or debate which common data model they should use for an integration project. Adding web services to the mix, they no longer need to build or debate which integration tool to use. Web services have been added to the water supply.

The Value Chain

When we step a little farther away from home, our horizons expand greatly. Crossing the organizational boundary with ACORD standards need no longer mean negotiating systems integration efforts with partners, or building consortia, or acquiring players elsewhere in the value chain. Put simply, by using ACORD's XML standards and web services, players can collaborate with each other rather than integrating. This means our systems, and the businesses they enable, can be more flexible in their dealings.

It's as if they have a simple visa allowing them to travel and do business anywhere. In the old world, you might need an army (of interpreters, if not always of soldiers) before you could establish a trading relationship in a distant territory – and you only learned of these foreign opportunities from the few intrepid explorers who made it home. That's how system-to-system communication used to happen outside the organization, before web services. You needed to have heard of a potential partner, and you needed an army of techies to get the systems talking with each other.

Web services allow pieces of functionality to discover each other and interoperate. Just as the web allowed us to learn easily about potential partners and customers in other industries and countries, so web services allow us to go to the next level and transact with them. Web services speaking ACORD XML standards are equipped to offer insurance services to other parties, whoever they are and wherever they are.

"You needed an army of techies to get the systems talking with each other." Virtual organizations and extended value chains now become much more viable than they were before. It's possible to construct business lines to exploit opportunities that simply don't appear on the less sensitive detection instruments of traditional businesses. The key concept is aggregation: aggregation of niche markets, of short-life situations, and of fragmented risks.

Aggregating Niches

One niche market that can be aggregated by a virtual organization is personal insurance. A consumer electronics supplier, acting with a lender and an insurer, can offer product-related finance packages to purchasers. Web services allow the three players to set up their cooperative

venture much more easily than before. Web services also allow the players to be more promiscuous than previously. Perhaps, for example, the lender in our scenario reserves the right to change insurers in mid-flight, unhooking the value chain from Insurer A and hooking it to Insurer B without any interruption of business service.

By implementing a flexible, virtual organization with web services, the players can also extend their offer. They might want to bring in a shipping service, a home repair and replacement service, and — given the interactive nature of most consumer electronics goods — a set of content suppliers. The list of value-adds is as long as your imagination.

Now this kind of sophisticated virtual organization has been made possible, where should we look for leadership in creating such services? I believe insurers, through their adoption of ACORD's XML standards, are well placed to inspire these extended services.

This kind of aggregation creates larger markets, but not necessarily personalized ones. To create a personalized version of this offer, we would need to add a richer understanding of the individual consumer as a determinant of the insurance element's terms and cost. Again, web services make such analyses much easier to perform. Demographic and psychodemographic data can be delivered from organizations operating web sites, call centers and other high-touch facilities.

> **"The list of value-adds is as long as your imagination."**

Moving to short-life opportunities, we can imagine real-time personalized insurance products that react to changes in the owner's state or whereabouts. A travel insurance product, for example, could remold its terms and benefits depending on the user's changing location. The user might input their location to a wireless PDA, by tapping on a map. More spookily, a network operator could use her cell phone signal to determine the cell the user is in, and transmit the information on to the insurer. It becomes possible to offer and withdraw product elements as users move across frontiers – some of which might be invisible to them.

Can insurers make money out of such opportunities? Someone will figure out how.

Pipe Dream to Faucet

There's more to ACORD's XML standards than meets the eye. That's because the standards aren't for your eyes only. They're also meant to be read, understood and processed by other systems. They're the key to engaging in flexible, value-added relationships that expand markets, optimize revenues and harvest opportunities otherwise lost to passing time. Standards give their users access to a networked, real-time business world populated by customers, partners and opportunities. ACORD's XML standards place a community-driven, domain-specific vocabulary in the neighborhood of all kinds of other businesses speaking the same broad language and open for business.

Are we indulging in pipe dreams? Vacationing in cloud cuckoo-land? Well, technologists call your Internet connection a pipe, and they call the network a cloud. The fact is, our business world has been changed by the arrival of the Internet, and it will be shaped further as Internet technologies, and the standards they bear, continue to mature. The net is a key part of the environment we inhabit. We need standards to get along in this environment, and if we embrace standards with creativity, we'll do better than getting along.

> "The Net is a key part of the environment we inhabit."

At ACORD, we're proud to be leading the adoption of standards in the insurance industry. We're determined to motivate our community to innovate: to build new services, new businesses, and new markets. We encourage you to see and use ACORD as your platform: your launch platform to innovation.

■

6

Customer Expectations

They're driving but who's navigating?

The Customer Is Always Right? Wrong.

Chris Whittle, the controversial founder of the Edison Schools project[13], argued in the early 1990s that the school system needed reinventing. He used Edison's breakthrough in electric lighting as a metaphor for the change in thinking he was advocating:

> We need a complete redesign of the way we teach our children.
> This means we cannot begin with the system we now have.
> When Edison invented electric illumination, he didn't tinker
> with candles to make them burn better. Instead he created
> something brilliantly new: the lightbulb.[14]

Whatever you may think of Whittle's for-profit schools, there's no denying the power (pun intended) of his founding metaphor. If Thomas Edison had relied on customer feedback as the driving force of his innovations, then he might have wound up making longer candles. It's lucky he didn't. Electric lighting has extended the working day, brought additional leisure time, and made our indoor environment safer. We wouldn't want to be without it.

In the same vein, the British comedian and media commentator Armando Ianucci once pointed out that if the Fox TV network had asked focus groups if people wanted to watch the animated adventures of a family with yellow skin and overbites, The Simpsons would never have been made.

Twenty-twenty hindsight is a great gift. It's easy to see today why the incandescent light bulb and the timeless city of Springfield are both winning concepts. We're used to them. They're part of the world we live in.

Customer thinking is rooted in the familiar. It's therefore tied to the past, not trained on the future. Customers focus on the present for many understandable reasons, not the least of which are financial. This means that depending solely on customer feedback can result in incremental improvement to your products or services at best, rather than any sort of breakthrough thinking.

> **"When customers are asked about future enhancements, they stay within their frames of reference."**

When customers are asked about future enhancements, they stay within their frames of reference. They ask for changes and enhancements to current products. I don't recall consumers lobbying hardware stores for garage door openers. There was no popular desire to walk around listening to music on headphones until some time after the boss of Sony demanded a way of listening to his own tapes on the numerous business flights he took.

Focus groups can also give very strong, but misleading, signals.

Sometimes the only valid data they produce comes about by accident: Philips once held a focus group to determine customer preference for radios. Participants mostly said they'd prefer a colored radio to a gray one, yet when they picked up radios offered to them as thanks for taking part, the designers noticed that most took the gray model.[15]

If innovative companies were guided only by consumers, thousands of products would never have been invented. That sounds like heresy, in an age when "customer focus" is the leading mantra of contemporary business orthodoxy. Pleasing the customer seems like the right thing to do, particularly in a service industry. Going above and beyond the call of duty to exceed customer expectations seems to make sound business sense.

Customers Are Often Wrong

But providing day-to-day service that exceeds customer expectations is different from asking customers for guidance when introducing new service concepts or building technology solutions. When it comes to innovation, the truth is the customer is not always right. In fact, customers can often be dead wrong, leading developers up blind alleys and destroying substantial investments in the process.

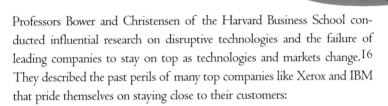

Professors Bower and Christensen of the Harvard Business School conducted influential research on disruptive technologies and the failure of leading companies to stay on top as technologies and markets change.[16] They described the past perils of many top companies like Xerox and IBM that pride themselves on staying close to their customers:

> While companies may think they are in control of their own destinies, customers have a powerful influence on the direction of company investments.

When launching new products, managers quickly look to customers. They assess need, market size, and potential return on investment. What does a vendor do when customers do not look favorably on a new product because it does not fit the present way of doing business?

"The truth is the customer is not always right."

Bower and Christensen believe "managers must beware of ignoring new technologies that don't initially meet the needs of their mainstream customers." They must address the "next-generation performance needs of their customers." In other words, they must look beyond feedback. They must look to the customers they don't yet have. Some of those customers will be entirely new customers, while others will be existing customers who acquire new needs, and new understandings of their needs.

The authors go on to say "it is nearly impossible to build a case for diverting resources from known customer needs in established markets to markets and customers that seem insignificant or do not yet exist." We've all been in this situation, where the attractiveness of the devil we know isn't in question, but the candidate replacements are unknown. The risks of changing market strategy are hard to measure. But too much emphasis on the customer's present needs "can blind you to new technologies in emerging markets."

The history of large, innovative projects also provides plenty of warnings against "no-brainer" changes where the rationale is based on presumed behavior changes by large groups of people. The Channel Tunnel between England and France opened in 1994 with forecasts of 15.9 million rail passengers. The actual figure turned out to be 2.9 million – a bare 18 percent of the forecast. By 2001, passenger numbers had climbed but only to 6.9 million.[17] By the way, while we're considering what it's like to redevelop a great old city, it's interesting to note that standards played a major role in the building of Boston:

> "Risks of changing market strategy are hard to measure."

> In 1689, the Boston city fathers recognized the need for standardization when they passed a law making it a civic crime to manufacture bricks in any size other than 9x4x4. The city had just been destroyed by fire, and the city fathers decided that standards would assure rebuilding in the most economic and fastest way possible.[18]

Incrementalism

But to return to the dangers of innovative projects.... There's a real dilemma for planners here. It's not surprising many people who should be looking at innovation retreat to incrementalism. When I ask technology vendors about the drag on innovation, the response usually involves maintaining and upgrading the installed base of customers. They're anxious to carry their customers with them – but they're not sure where they're ultimately going. Customers, on the other hand, naturally seek to maximize their investment in technology and avoid running the upgrade gauntlet. Agents, for example, typically want to see the added value of a system before they increase their investment. Since system changes can be disruptive, there is a natural disincentive to move forward. Conversions and upgrades can gobble up precious time and resources when the business can least afford it – even though the newest technologies are making it easier to modify and integrate systems.

> "Customers seek to maximize their investment in technology."

The result is a tension between vendors who want to innovate – while being unable to quantify the risks of innovation – and their mainstream customers who want their current systems to run smoothly. The vendors' dilemma is embodied in the technology trade shows. The large general shows focus on innovation, with many new and prototype products in the "Gee-Whiz" category. Events aimed at the insurance industry tend to deliver information about current products and upgrades. The difference in the two types of event is like the gap between the big auto shows, with their shiny concept cars, and your local car showroom with its array of "this year's models." How does the average buyer bridge the gap between a vision for the future, and the products that are currently safe to manufacture in volume?

Standards Close the Gap

Standards, in the form of legislation or industry agreement, can play an important part in narrowing the gap, or resolving the tension, between innovation and expectation. If, for example, the federal government were to introduce laws governing vehicle emissions, then fuel-efficient electric and hybrid cars would appear in our showrooms. In the same way, when government departments – and large corporations – mandate that suppliers deal with them electronically for purchasing, their partners in the supply chain have to get on board, or exit the market.

> "The pressure to innovate is not going to come from the mainstream of users."

The pressure to innovate is not going to come from the mainstream of users. Users can grow accustomed to using bad software products and some even learn to love them. But not keeping up with technology's increasing ability to support business operations can be as dangerous as always riding the leading edge.

These are challenging times for technology vendors that pride themselves on being responsive to their customers. Will listening to their customers be their undoing? Not if they can please mainstream customers and, at the same time, manage emerging products customers may not immediately accept. In fact, Bower and Christensen assert mainstream and disruptive businesses cannot be managed in a single organization since the mainstream operation will tend to dominate. They recommend a separate independent operation or group for new products.

One example of this separation is found at Sony, where the Playstation games console was conceived and developed in California without any involvement from head office in Japan. Even Sony, the inventors of so many breakthrough consumer electronics products we take for granted today, has to protect its innovative efforts from the drag effect of its mainstream success.

> **"Vendors created products for emerging markets long before the customers were ready to buy."**

You don't need to look far to find vendors that created products for emerging markets long before the customers were ready to buy. In the end, it seems timing will be the key. Vendors need to anticipate need and precede or create the market, but not too soon. Premature deployment depletes capital. However, late deployment loses market share and runs the risk that newer technologies could make the new product obsolete.

There are real risks involved in innovation, and in standing still. But one thing is certain: If you miss the technology wave that raises your line of business to a new level, then you're out of the game altogether. You can absorb the punches technology failures will bring you, because you can limit the business's exposure to technologies that are in an immature state. But you can't buy back your place at the table if you get left behind when the game moves to a brand new town.

Changing Environments Change Customers

We're used to the idea technologies emerge from laboratories, increase in scale and infiltrate our lives in an almost mechanical fashion. It's as if they evolve of their own accord, and then exist for our use. In this view of social development, technologies are neutral. The first hammer has no moral weight: man decides whether he'll use it to build a shelter or brain his neighbor.

But there's no doubt the appearance of new technologies in our midst radically changes our options. The hammer creates a new moral choice, and a legion of potential new industries. Technologies are anything but neutral from the point of view of how things turn out on our little planet. And every technology we have created has changed our world, often by removing barriers that were previously regarded as "natural." For example, the simple electric lightbulb allowed people to read in the evenings, and enabled workplaces to become larger. So the lightbulb was, amongst other things, a tool of literacy and productivity. Two simple barriers that had stood firm through the long development of our society – the availability of natural light, and the cost of reliable artificial light – were swept away in an instant.

Communications technologies have some of the greatest effects on the opportunities open to us. The ability to call people on the other side of the world, or to catch a plane and go visit them, has completely transformed the way we structure our economies and the way we think about the planet. Some environmentalists think the pictures of the earth transmitted from the Apollo missions radically altered people's understanding of the planet we share and our responsibility for its upkeep. And clearly, car ownership has shaped the way we have built our communities.

I mention these technologies in particular because the technologies of travel are often left out of discussions of communications networks, in favor of the telecoms networks that are so radically altering our landscape in

"Each technological change has affected the insurance business."

the present generation. Yet travel is at the heart of communications. The channels we create, whether or not they are electronic channels, destroy distance. They bring us together. They let us all travel to find new places, new people and new ideas. And they let us distribute our products and services to entirely new market opportunities. The proliferation of channels – in the wake of any new communications technology – changes the world at a fundamental level.

We sometimes forget the history of the insurance industry is built on the evolution of distribution channels. In the 1700s, you had to visit an insurance company office to purchase insurance. It was a local business. A developing postal system allowed companies to appoint independent agents, who could sell and make decisions while still communicating with the home office through written messages. The growth of direct writing companies parallels the development of mass communications capabilities in this nation, beginning with the advent of radio networks in the 1920s through 1940s and the subsequent launch of television networks in the 1950s.

Telephones were in just about every American home by the 1950s. Mass marketing became possible and cost effective. Telemarketing was launched. Each technological change in the way we distribute information has affected the insurance business, and the automation revolution will continue to put pressure on us to adapt the way we reach our customers.

And it's not just the primary effect of technologies that changes markets. The way technologies impact other industries affects the way customers interact with ours. The insurance business can't – and shouldn't try to – insulate itself from changed goals and expectations brought about by our customers' experiences with other service providers.

For example, telephone and online banking lead consumers to expect all kinds of financial products may be sold through electronic channels. They may latch on to this idea because these channels are efficient and low-cost routes to simple services. The insurance professional isn't going to see a natural parallel between an ATM dispensing bills and balances, and an agent quoting for a policy. These are, from the provider's point of view, entirely dissimilar services. Yet the customer, with his layman's viewpoint, creates a challenge. If there is no obvious equivalent in insurance to the ATM, then what is the non-obvious equivalent?

Expectations

We need to unpack the customer's modified expectations – the changed attitude he has gained toward financial channels as a result of using ATMs. What benefits does the bank's ATM give him? The machine allows him to get cash at whatever time suits him, without having to join a line in the banking hall or wait until the bank is open. He can check his balance too, and run various other simple housekeeping functions. The ATM takes the routine functions of retail banking, and puts them conveniently on the outside wall or in the lobby, bringing increased convenience to the customer's life while reducing some of the bank's clerical costs.

In the insurance business, the routine functions that eat up clerical costs are many and varied, but a large number of them relate to quite small customer transactions. Reporting the value of a policy, for example, is similar to reporting a checking account balance. With customers now used to the ease with which banks can report balances, they now expect insurers to produce valuations on demand as well. It may not make sense to build a specialized machine to do this, but an online function can certainly achieve what's needed. Other high-volume routine functions, such as vehicle collision claims, are already being transformed by the use of digital cameras and wireless devices, so that information from the scene of the event is fed directly into the relevant backend systems. Customers know the technologies to support this activity exist, since they own and use the gadgets themselves. And if they're in any doubt about the devices' use in business, they'll be quickly disabused next time they move home, and their realtor is using similar equipment.

Customers' expectations are their standards. Innovative customer service in one industry raises the bar for all industries, because the bar exists in customers' minds.

The standards used by the providers also perform this function of declaring expectations. Standards set a boundary around the ambitions of the communities that use them. Imagine a community of mixed language speakers decides it will only use a common vocabulary of 200 words. The community will make initial gains in efficiency, because its members will be able to converse within the bounds set by the vocabulary. Soon, however, they will run out of new ideas. Unless they can coin new words, and new ways of assembling words into conversations, their culture will suffer. Many industries traditionally act in this way, sticking to the first "dictionaries" agreed by their founders.

Industries can only keep pace with developments in their environments if they cultivate their own vocabularies. This means growing their word-hoard, and pruning it of dead wood. It means keeping a watchful eye on the relevance and coverage of the standards they use to communicate. And it means committing to representing all the voices that operate within the community — and the voices of those who are lining up to join the community or challenge its power.

> "Industries can only keep pace with developments in their environments if they cultivate their own vocabularies."

Customers are major actors in our business environment. They adapt rapidly to certain types of new technology and, in particular, communications networks. They also absorb and transfer expectations across industry dividing lines. Customers therefore make up a strong source of, and force for, change. But it's as if we've misread the customer's role in change. We expect customers to dictate innovation through explicit means, like focus groups – when, as we have seen, their conscious focus is on the present and past, not the future. At the same time, we dismiss the deeper changes in behavior customers signal to us via their defections or service complaints, or their apparently unreasonable comparisons with other industries. It's these messages we should be listening to, and decoding. This is where we're going to hear the first articulations of the future.

R/evolution

Has the Internet brought revolution, or evolution? This argument continues to play out wherever people gather to talk about the changing business environment. People who have been badly emotionally burned in the collapse of the dotcom bubble sometimes choose to dismiss the argument out of hand. But unless you're in a state of  chronic denial, you have to admit the Internet cannot be disinvented, or torn out of the world it has infiltrated. It is part of our lives, and of our businesses. Its effects will continue to impact the way we behave and the decisions we make.

Which side is right? Both are.

Distribution

There was a time when distribution was less complicated than it is today. Now everyone is wondering about the longevity of established distribution channels, particularly as new electronic channels become more prevalent. Today, it is not uncommon for insurers – or businesses in general – to maintain and manage multiple access points. Customers can do business in person, by mail, by telephone with operators or voice response telephony systems, or by personal computer. Add the option to purchase products directly, through agents or as a by-product of buying other products, and the number of potential distribution and service channel permutations can be mind-boggling.

Will the Internet wipe out all these other channels? Don't count on it. We've been here before, and history tells us that new channels increase overall activity.

For example, radio didn't kill theater, but it changed the direction of the theater toward more challenging material radio could not carry, and also toward the kind of musical extravaganza only the live theater can create. Television didn't kill radio, but forced it to evolve into an array of differentiated offerings, from shock-jock-led talk stations to easy-listening, drive-time all-the-time FM stations. If you want to reach back to the dawn of media, you could say writing didn't make talking obsolete.

So it has proven with the Internet technologies. The Web didn't destroy TV or magazines, and contrary to all rational expectations its biggest effect so far may be its contribution to the sale of books and the use of public libraries. Online banking is a useful service, but it's an additive service that lines up alongside the ATM and counter service to improve the bank's service. Retailers who followed the "clicks-and-bricks" approach to their online ventures have fared better than their pure-play online competitors. Webvan, for example, folded not because online groceries are a poor idea – customers love them – but because dedicated warehousing and supply networks are ruinously expensive. In Europe, the online arm of leading supermarket Tesco happily delivers groceries regularly to masses of customers who order online and pay delivery charges – using its existing base of stores, warehouses, trucks and enterprise systems.

> " A 'clicks-and-bricks' approach fared better than their pure-play online competitors. "

Banks Are not Closing Branches

Most bank customers have ATM cards, but banks are not closing all their expensive branches. While self-service oriented banking customers appreciate having the ability to access services through multiple channels – using a telephone or computer for bill payments, fund transfers, and account information – banks are finding high-tech options do not displace other access points. Branches are viewed positively by consumers for a number of reasons, including their desire to talk with someone in person to resolve a problem or to process more complicated transactions like loans, mortgages, and investments. And banks are learning that without branches they have fewer opportunities to build genuine relationships with their customers, and to sell them new products and services.

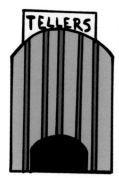

Although many customers do business by mail, telephone, and computer, Fidelity and Schwab investment centers have opened on highways in just about every major city throughout the United States. Like banks, these investment centers are trying to focus more on sales rather than service. Opening accounts, explaining products and providing advice on a growing number of options seems to be the strategy, and personally solving customers' problems as well. In essence, the face-to-face experience continues to be a valued channel for sales and for the beginning of a business relationship. Other less personal channels tend to be widely accepted for ongoing customer service.

Great as it is, you still can't get a cup of coffee at Amazon.com. You can read what other customers think of the products on offer, but you can't mingle with them. Buying online is an intellectual experience that is efficient and pleasurable in its own way. But it is not the sum total of human experience.

"Consumers place high value on alternative delivery options."

The cashless and checkless society has a way to go to displace more traditional channels of banking. According to US Banker magazine in a study conducted by Dove Associates, a Boston-based consulting firm for banking, "older and lower-income consumers prefer branches." In fact they conclude "even technology and convenience-driven consumers place value on the branch channel... Consumers place high value on alternative delivery options, [but] the need for personal service will continue to be an important part of what consumers look for in their banking experience." They conclude the customer indeed "does want everything."

We can look at many of these observations and studies in the banking and financial services industry and apply them to insurance. And while the pundits suggest (and I believe they are correct) that it is unlikely for an individual organization or representative to single-handedly sell and service property-casualty insurance, life insurance, mutual funds, stocks, options, commodities, mortgages and other loans and investments, the lines have blurred somewhat when you consider the appetite for mergers and acquisitions among the global financial services conglomerates. Fashions in mergers and acquisitions come and go, but the concept of "the one-stop financial shop" never goes away. While no single person may sell us a basket of such services, you can be sure these professionals are going to do all they can, within the framework of the laws and regulations, to bundle services in some way.

Multiple Channel Distribution

The challenge is to build and manage a multiple-channel distribution network to sell and service a variety of products to meet the needs of our customers today and tomorrow. Personal relationships will continue to be important while customers will expect electronic channels to improve quality and speed of service while providing access anytime, anywhere.

> **"Personal relationships will continue to be important."**

It's a tall order. The industry isn't going to fulfill the dream overnight. If we're experiencing a revolution, then it's a rolling revolution. If, on the other hand, we're living through an evolution, it's an evolution we must guide. In either case, our greatest responsibility is to recognize, encourage and nurture ideas. Ideas provide the light we need to grow, and to see ahead.

Edison's lightbulb has been appearing in cartoons as shorthand for "idea" for longer than anyone can remember. Did an earlier generation of cartoonists draw candles above their characters' heads? I guess not. The light Edison brought to our world was bright, clean — and sudden. It's a disruptive light that illuminates the shadows, a light that creates new space, and that carves new time from the encroaching night.

Let me add a further twist and ask you this: How many lightbulbs will it take to change your business?

7

Celebrate Your Seams

Building the best information capability

This chapter is about how enterprises can build an information systems capability more than equal to the tough demands of today's business environment – and the even tougher demands tomorrow will bring.

The ideas presented here are from the mainstream of the software engineering discipline, but they are not often presented in an accessible form to decision-makers. And they are all-too-often lost in the marketing and technical discourse surrounding the software industry.

I hope you'll find these ideas chime with your own views on business systems, and that they help to strengthen your resolve to deliver the best value you can to your customers.

Seamlessness

How many times have you heard the term "seamless" used to describe a system process? This adjective has an almost irresistible appeal to software marketers. And it plays to one of the deepest desires of technology buyers: that a system will fit in with other systems, and not require us to alter our existing systems to accommodate it.

"Specialized objects that can all collaborate to get the work of the enterprise done."

Unfortunately, the pursuit of seamlessness is a kind of folly. The finest business system teams *celebrate* their seams. They can't get enough of them.

A seam is an interface: a place where two objects meet and cooperate. Your systems capability needs to be composed of many specialized objects that can all collaborate to get the work of the enterprise done. You can think of your "systems" as a million tiny systems, or as one big system. But it makes most sense to think of your information capability as a portfolio of useful, collaborating objects that – in certain configurations – deliver business goals.

At its simplest, we can imagine having a rating engine as a common service to many virtual "systems" within the portfolio. We invest in a robust and reliable rating service we can then hook up, rather like a power source, to other objects needing to use it. The other objects might be customer application handlers, documentation producers and billing engines.

Components

Note the objects (or components, or services) we're talking about here can either be described like specialized people (handlers, producers, managers, agents and so on) or engines. In all cases we're positing "black boxes" that do very specific jobs.

The mainstream of the software engineering profession is now focused acutely on realizing this vision of a service-based IT architecture. The phrase "Web services" is the current term for this movement, but it's also been called "object technology" and "component computing." In fact, Web services subsume these earlier movements and extend them, so there is an intellectual backwards-compatibility at work here.

In a service-based architecture, various data transformations are bundled as meaningful chunks of business process, and made available as simple utilities. We can "plug in" a rating engine, or a workflow framework, or any other kind of service when we need it.

We no longer buy or build successive stovepipe solutions that repeat common functions. Nor do we limit ourselves to one "enterprise solution" enabling every business function we might ever need but from one supplier only.

In effect, we create a highly standardized market within the systems function. There are several ways to define and stock an information capability of this kind. The techniques I favor can be traced back to some of the pioneering work in the object technology field.

Take, for example, the technique called Responsibility Driven Design. This is an approach to defining collaborating components focusing on what each component is meant to do, what it delivers to other components, and what it expects from other components with which it interacts. It's a way of defining the interface to a component without necessarily descending to program code level.

Responsibilities can be defined as contracts. A contract specifies a service provided by a component. In the real world, a contract might specify an airline will carry a customer from New York to Los Angeles on a particular flight at a particular price, as long as the customer presents himself at the right terminal, in good time for the flight, and with baggage weighing below a set level. In systems terms, a contract might specify a rating engine will produce a commercial premium in a defined format in return for a customer identifier, risk category and product code.

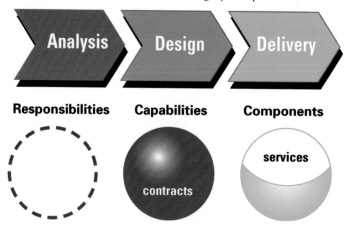

Figure 7: Developing Services

By focusing on responsibilities, we can define the enterprise's information capabilities in terms of investments and business value. Defining responsibilities is akin to throwing a boundary around an area of business concern. Responsibilities can be used to define information capabilities; and capabilities can be realized in software as components.

Once we have built a production approach to deliver capabilities through components, it becomes easy to manage the business systems mission as a portfolio activity. Your components are your portfolio assets. The capabilities your components represent are your investment criteria. So, you might have a handful of components collaborating to deliver customer information to frontline staff members. Each of the underlying capabilities in the set embodies an aspect of your strategy for customer service, and your attitude to customer relationships. It's now much easier to relate the technology streaming into the day-to-day activity of the business with the enterprise's goals. You're no longer trying to compare sheep with corn, but are using the common currency of capabilities to ensure business concepts and system processes can be translated one with the other. This is a key leap forward for business/IT alignment.

An Architecture Mindset

Creating this kind of service-based, capability-focused architecture is partly a matter of mindset. Once you accept the standards-driven mindset, the sense of this architecture rapidly becomes clear. What we've done is squeeze out the notion of autonomous behavior or bi-directional relationships and replace them with the expectation disparate parties will achieve larger tasks by working together.

When a vendor asks you to believe his solution will serve all your needs, he is asking you to fall back to an earlier stage of evolution in which autonomous decisions made sense. When you are sold "systems integration" you are (more often than not) being sold bi-directional relationships. But you know the growth in complexity and reach of the business demands you build flexibility and reconfigurability into your systems capability. The only way you can do this with any confidence is to regard the systems capability as a kit of parts. And the only way a kit of parts can produce usable and reusable pieces of business service is if the kit is standards-based.

8

The Digital Divide

Closing the business/technology gap

Pundits often talk about a "digital divide" between "haves" and "have-nots" in modern society. But there is also a divide between IT and the business it serves. And I have spent almost my entire career in the middle, working both sides of the aisle.

In the early 1970s, I joined the Methods and Systems group at Chubb because I understood the business as well as the technology. I worked with end-users (business people) to better understand their needs so I could also work with highly skilled technicians developing software. If I did my job right, we built what the business needed.

Thirty years later I am essentially doing the same thing, closing the gap between the business and technology. Technology has become increasingly complex and changes so rapidly business people often have a difficult time understanding how it can best serve their needs today. And creative software developers often lack a real understanding of the business itself. But those firms that can close this gap are building great companies.

The Fabric of Business

CEOs often say their business is about managing money and not much else matters. Others say it's about product and pricing. But, in my opinion, technology has become so inextricably interwoven into the fabric of our business today I fail to see how we can attract capital and craft innovative products at competitive prices without it. Whether one is attracting investors with a low-cost infrastructure and high returns or appealing to customers, IT is a key enabler. Although it was a financial market calamity more than an effect of misguided or misused technology, the Bubble only compounded a long-standing problem for those of us in the middle.

Some view IT as a series of failed investments with no significant return. The adage of "over-promise and under-deliver" still beckons many senior executives. But it would be wrong to conclude the IT investment was misguided. Technology is not created in a vacuum nor does it function independent of the business process itself.

Firms also need to recognize the way they do business must change as well. Unfortunately, the generalizations about IT in our business contain just enough truth to evolve into folklore of sorts. And the problem with such half-truths is they give rise to perceptions and attitudes among senior executives that influence and shape corporate strategy, for better or for worse. I've seen them all.

Reasons for business anxieties about technology vary and reliable metrics are difficult to come by. We hear speakers take the stage and say if the automobile had advanced as much as the computer over the past few decades, a car would cost one dollar and travel thousands of miles on fuel cells costing only pennies. This implies the cost of computing and communicating data have dropped precipitously, and continue to do so. But that really doesn't matter, does it? The key is to leverage the power of lower cost computing to innovate your business. IT is the enabler, the tool. And modern tools in the hands of craftsmen can create wonders.

Ease of Doing Business

Today, more than ever, customers choose among equals based on "ease of doing business." The value of an insurance contract is not the only factor to be considered. In fact, it may become the least important in some ways. You need not look very far beyond your own consumer products experience to validate this statement. Services built around products that have been around for a while are commonplace. The insurance industry can provide innovative services (risk management, claims and others) as part of standard insurance products and building these solutions will be enabled by various technologies.

I remember the days when ACORD members only viewed standards from a cost containment perspective. Today, our ability to easily move information has become a competitive necessity as well. Our business is all about partnerships and alliances and this means it is also about sharing and moving information.

> **"Today, our ability to easily move information has become a competitive necessity as well."**

Changing what we do and how we think is a far more difficult challenge than the technology itself. But we have a bounty of new generation tools to reduce software development time from years to days and platforms connecting almost everyone on the planet, instantly. Couple the new hardware and software advances with open industry standards for moving information (such as ACORD's) and you can create compelling new business models, even in mature and highly regulated industries.

Uncouple technology strategy from business strategy and you have a dead business. Perhaps you have seen some dead businesses today, but "they just don't know they're dead" as Haley Joel Osment said to Bruce Willis in the movie *The Sixth Sense*. So the question to ask is not how to deploy technology to build a great business. The question to ask is: How do people who build great businesses see and use technology differently than you do? That's where you'll find the real difference between the winners and the losers.

The Expectations Curve

We met Carlota Perez's Surge model of technological/economic change in Chapter 1. The Expectations Curve is a close relative of this model, focusing on the difference between the growing capability of a technology and the expectations attached to it.

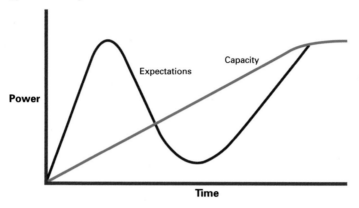

Figure 8: The Expectations Curve

Notice how expectations build to an unrealistic peak before slumping back again. We're familiar with this pattern from technology introductions over the years. Our hopes and fears are loaded on to one particular technology – such as the Internet or biotechnology – and projections outstrip current capability.

But note also how the backlash over-compensates for earlier enthusiasm. We're in this dip at the present time, with regard to Internet technologies. Sentiment has it the Internet is no good for anything – whereas its real power continues to increase. Some commentators identify this "dip" period as the window of opportunity. This is where people who can harness the true capability of a technology can over-deliver on expectations. They are also less likely to be distracted by media froth and market frenzy.

Small Angles, Big Distances: The Properties Of Divergence

The Chinese proverb says: "The journey of a thousand miles begins with a single step." I'd like to add a caveat: It also helps if you're going in the right direction.

Sometimes people tell me standards can't be very important, since the differences they seek to remove are, in many cases, tiny. Does it really matter if my business defines a customer address differently than yours? The two objects won't be so different we'll mistake them for entirely different areas of knowledge. Isn't there room for a little slack here?

If "fuzzy matching" really did apply in business – let alone in business systems – then I'd agree with this statement. We'd accept a degree of wiggle room in how our businesses interacted with each other, and let some kind of automated common sense solve any misunderstandings.

But that's assuming our systems have some kind of sentient power – some independent source of reasoning. But our systems are not self-conscious. They do not "understand" the world they appear to animate in their functionality. Our systems are only working models of chunks of business. No more, and no less.

Allow your standards to lapse and your systems will start to produce gibberish. You know the other proverb: Garbage In, Garbage Out. Well, the line between good data and garbage is as thin – and as strong – as the wrapper of a sound business standard.

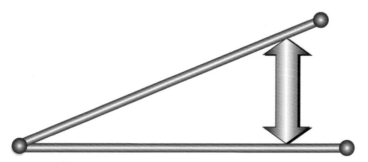

Figure 9: Small Angles, Big Distances

Even a small angle of difference will create a large gap if divergent paths are left to develop.

You only need to be a little off in your alignment, and the addition of time will produce a massive difference in the orientation of the business and its information capability. Fortunately, there are steps you can take to close the gap. I submit it's the responsibility of technology folks to take these actions. Notice how each of the actions involves thinking like the business:

Reduce The Divide By Closing The Angle

- Replace technical jargon with an emphasis on the business language of standards.
- Put all project goals in business language and relate explicitly to business goals.
- Do joint scenario work with the business.
- Describe and evaluate business systems as a managed portfolio of assets.

One of the reasons divergence occurs is it's hard to get an overview of the current situation while it's taking place. In the midst of the battle, it can be hard to judge who's winning. Similarly, any active organization can look chaotic on a snapshot basis. Thankfully, standards provide a context to make sense of current activities. They act as a roadmap to which everyone in the enterprise can refer.

The Standards Gap

Making Progress?

- Activities within an organization often look chaotic.
- Analyzing the activities will show you how they connect up, and expose any that don't contribute to your goals.
- Successful strategy isn't a straight line to your goals. Your progress will deviate according to the obstacles you meet and communications failures.
- Standards supply a framework for analyzing your business.
- The process of creating and implementing standards follows the same logic: progress rarely appears smooth and continuous at any one point of observation.

Signs of a Standards Gap

1. Clerical teams embark on regular data conversion exercises.

2. Exceptions have become enshrined in workarounds.

3. The organization is locked into unusual technologies and a diminishing supply of resources for maintenance.

4. Change requests for improvements to process take too long.

5. Training is organization-specific, very customized and expensive to deliver.

6. There is little flexibility among staff members as systems are too dissimilar.

7. The organization has a static-to-shrinking pool of business partners.

8. The product set is aging, expensive to update and inflexible making it difficult to tailor to meet customer needs.

9. Percentage of resources allocated to maintenance or basic projects is in the 70% to 85% range leaving less than 15% to 20% for strategic projects; less than half what other financial services organizations commit.

10. There is no one in the organization responsible for the business information standards.

There's another way of defining the digital divide, and that's in terms of the extent to which standards have been used to tie business and IT into a common goal set. There are ten major symptoms of the standards gap, and I've listed them on the opposite page.

And the remedy for the standards gap? Adopting standards!

CIO Touchstones

- Hire, develop and retain the best people available. This is easy to say but hard to do in today's marketplace. And it won't get any easier.
- Breed a positive attitude by building on accomplishments and not criticizing the user every step of the way.
- Develop a positive relationship between yourself and other executives so associates in IT and other departments get along together.
- Develop a sales personality within the department so the IT team is viewed as both forward-looking thinkers and committed, pragmatic realists. The good CIO is a walking ad for the professionalism of his people.
- Provide and encourage opportunities for staff to keep current on technology developments, so the organization remains at the forefront of potential opportunities.
- Be the focal point in the organization for the application of technology and its business benefits, including emerging uses and techniques.
- Be a "hands-on" executive with a real appreciation of what it takes to get the job done.
- Build a reputation as someone who delivers on your promises.

Why do IT projects fail? Why are they delivered late? Why do they so rarely meet the expectations set for them?

The blame for IT failures gets laid at the door of the CIO. And CIOs are big enough folks to take the knocks. But knocking the IT leadership isn't going to help matters. When IT fails, we all fail. Every late or unsuccessful project I've experienced and examined has been due to a collaborative failure of all the organizational participants.

Successful technology implementation requires the executive management team to buy in to the project and provide the support and resources it needs, from whichever areas of the corporation are affected. Otherwise, the project will not deliver the results the company needs.

"We wouldn't manage any other area of the business in such a cavalier fashion."

The CEO who plans to use technology as a strategic tool must have a basic knowledge of what it requires to develop a system, and especially appreciate the development cycle of any major initiative.

Skimping on understanding the process leads to anxiety, suspicion and disgruntlement when projects go wrong. We wouldn't manage any other area of the business in such a cavalier fashion.

Top management must facilitate IT success by dedicating skilled resources from both the business units involved and the IT department. The key determinants of business success are rarely technology competences or hardware investments. The high-impact factors lie in the nature of the business processes being tackled. Without insightful analysis of existing processes and skillful modeling of new processes, we can't create a real business blueprint for the system. Without a blueprint, we haven't got a workable solution.

The target users of the system play a central role in the development of any successful system. Requirements and specifications must be meticulously defined by the user. The system must be comprehensively tested by the user before it goes into production.

The Boss

The CEO must trust and communicate with the CIO on a frequent basis. For his part, the CIO must have detailed knowledge of the organization's operational units, and be able to talk at a business level. CEOs shouldn't have to listen to bits and bytes, or vendor jargon. They should be clear on what the development project is going to ask of the organization, and what the overall impact will be.

The implication is CEOs must commit time and interest to understanding the IT process. They must position IT at the same level of strategic attention dedicated to business areas such as marketing, manufacturing and finance. And since IT affects all the other functions in the business, the CEO should actually be more knowledgeable about IT than other strategic business units.

> "The CEO should actually be more knowledgeable about IT than other strategic business units."

If you expect great returns from your systems investment, you must cultivate and develop the IT mentality of the CEO. This is the challenge for CIOs today. It means guiding the exposure of the CEO to selected sales presentations of new concepts and ideas. It means accompanying the CEO to presentations and interpreting for him where necessary. It means achieving a balance between introducing new technology and systems concepts to the CEO in usable chunks and protecting him from the oversold or over-simplified pitches that plague him — from both inside and outside the organization.

By communicating effectively and regularly with the CEO, the CIO can manage expectations while filtering the application projects representing greatest opportunity to the enterprise. With the CEO on board, IT becomes strategic and support for funding and staffing becomes shared across the business.

The Business Share

Once a project has been approved, the IT team needs the support of the business units affected or served by the application. These units must allocate the same quality and quantity of resources to an IT project as they would to any other initiative in their area. Traditionally the business units don't dedicate staff to the project, and their IT expectations are not realized. Seconded staff members are usually too involved in their own business unit's work to commit the necessary time to the IT project. They may have a large list of other projects to complete for their own business unit, and these are generally assigned a higher priority.

> **"A major flaw is unrealistic expectations on the part of the user."**

One of the major flaws in today's IT stems from unrealistic expectations on the part of the user, particularly semi-committed user representatives. Every business unit has a list of system capabilities it would like, and it's true you can do virtually anything with software. But IT does not have infinite people resources. You can buy the hardware to meet the computing power needs, but the human talent is much less readily available. IT development productivity continues to improve, but business requirements will always outpace our human resources capability.

This is why I warn technology leaders not to bypass the CEO or the affected business units when looking for corporate backing for an initiative. A direct appeal to a point solution can never override the business's other problems and opportunities, sight unseen. If a project sneaks into the development schedule in this way, it will damage other projects. How many "number one" priorities can you have? Vision may be limitless, but resources are finite.

One answer to this problem is to hire outside contractors. However, unless these resources bring a fundamental knowledge of the insurance business and have deep and relevant applications knowledge of the business, then hiring them is identical to hiring new trainees. You'll get smart people, but not the breadth, depth and relevance of experience you need for a successful result.

Today's CIO spends a great deal of time building relationships with business executives and working with them as a team to develop business solutions. IT provides an opportunity to streamline and enrich the processes by which a customer deals with the firm. And the Internet revolution has generated higher customer expectations regarding the ease of doing business.

For his part, the CEO must have realistic expectations of IT, and assess the IT team's capability in the same way as he would his groups in marketing, underwriting or claims.

Systems Chemistry

I sometimes hear blanket statements about the inability of IT to deliver the functionality our industry requires. These statements usually project gloomily out over a three- or five-year period, and tend to imply all IT investment is ultimately wasted.

But these predictions are as vague in their premises as they are certain in their outcomes. Perhaps the people who make them are just reacting against software industry hype, or protecting their own areas of expertise. But if you define your objectives, align them with a rational analysis of what can be achieved, and then apply them in a realistic process, you can harness IT to massive business benefit. It doesn't have to go wrong.

The CEO's main responsibility is to be a coach and plan winning strategies that positively affect the bottom line. He must select the right players to execute the corporate business strategy in each area of the business and insure they work together. He focuses on matching and beating the company's competitors.

The CEO cannot be the focal point for every IT decision, involved in selecting software and hardware or ruling on development methods. He shouldn't be able to match a fellow CEO on nuts-and-bolts details of their respective systems, any more than he should carry a detailed opinion on marketing's latest propensity model or the color of the coffee coming out of the machines in Claims.

> **"The CEO cannot be the focal point for every IT decision."**

Too much interference by a CEO who is not knowledgeable in how systems are designed, how they are linked to other systems, and how they really fulfill the business need can only impact a project negatively. The CEO needs to keep personal preferences out of IT systems.

For an IT shop to be successful, the CIO must have business knowledge, skills, and understanding so he can determine the needs of the business and define application systems with the best bottom-line benefit to the organization. The CIO must build consensus among the management team as to the benefits of any system. He must obtain business unit commitment for continued support and high quality staffing to assist in the project development.

The Team

The key to success on any project is assembling the right team of people. The CIO must nurture the team so members get along, work together, make their best contribution, carry their load and develop their own potential.

Above all, the CIO needs to set a realistic and well defined project scope with objectives as well as a timetable of target dates so all members of the team are positive about the "doability" of the project. Committing to unrealistic schedules is a major factor in the failure of projects.

Any project demands solid project management throughout the time cycle of development. The CIO and his senior staff members can bring targeted expertise and assistance to bear in this area. This means the CIO and senior figures must know about the business process being tackled as well as the application development approach. Working with projects in this way is a good way of ensuring senior staff members keep their focus on business and management issues, so the tools of technology are applied with greatest effectiveness.

Once upon a time, an enterprise's technologists lived in a sealed, glass-walled room, and wore white coats. They punched cards and fed them into machine readers. They sent wheeled carts bearing stacks of reports around the office.

They lived in their own world. The business didn't understand them, or depend on them. A dropped punched card never sent a company spiraling out of business.

> "A dropped punched card never sent a company spiraling out of business."

We now live in a new era where technology is an integral part of the business process. The computers are on our desks, and in our pockets — and connected to other computers around the globe. In this world, poor technology decisions can lead to dire consequences. Bad IT decisions can destroy long-established enterprises.

The time when senior officers could maintain a hands-off relationship with IT are long gone.

Short IT Budgets

Researchers at Gartner Group put the annual worldwide spend on IT at $2.7 trillion. Perhaps as astonishing is their estimate that 20 percent of that spend is wasted. Clearly, keeping pace with the IT investment and targeting it wisely is a growing responsibility. Shaving dollars in IT, or sending those dollars in the wrong direction, can kill your business.

There is increased evidence that shortchanging IT budgets can be disastrous in our information-intensive, service-oriented industry. With technology lifespans shortening rapidly and manual costs continuing to climb, enterprises must innovate continually. IT's share of the business's total expenses is therefore growing, as for example in the brokerage community.

Keeping pace with technology development is a growing issue for many boards – and the task hasn't been helped by the distractions of the dotcom bubble. One insurer I know has an IT governing board composed of the top executives in the corporation. They find this a great way of keeping the business in sync with the capabilities of technology. Of course, you need a centralized or federated corporate IT infrastructure if your business is to benefit from this kind of creative focus. However you achieve it, technology must be managed across the organization rather than left to isolated departmental initiatives.

"The central role of technology in business affects us all."

The central role of technology in business affects us all. Technology impacts our businesses and our lives, professionally and personally. Unless you're a senior executive close to cashing-out, you have no choice but to be involved. If you're a CEO, you need to understand what's at stake when technology issues are discussed. It's not a matter of delegation or getting rid of the CIO if he doesn't deliver. By that time your goose might well be cooked.

And as business systems start to be defined and commissioned in terms of business process, via component technologies like J2EE and .Net, the reasons for committed participation from the CEO and top executives become more ever more acute. The gap between business problem and technical solution is being collapsed by these new service-based technologies. Many of our members attend executive programs conducted by IBM and other firms in order to stay on track with technology developments, and the opportunities new IT is creating for businesses of all kinds.

The Mandate For Change

The progress in technology over the past two decades has been staggering. Who would have thought the PC — an early 1980s toy useful for not much more than running spreadsheets — would be connected to every other PC in the world a mere fifteen years later? Or that teenagers would tote inexpensive mobile communications devices packing more processing power than the Apollo missions?

And yet the applications available to run our businesses are still too complex, difficult to maintain, and lacking in interoperability. If I asked you to describe your systems in terms of organizational rigidity or agility, what score would you give them? Almost all people respond that IT has created more rigidity in the way we do business today. At the same time, we know we need more agile organizations to deal with a faster and broader business world.

People frustrated with technology want to believe some organization, or some champion figure, should force vendors to deliver the systems we really need, or perhaps select a single solution from those available and mandate compliance across the industry. Governments, regulatory agencies, and nonprofit trade associations come in for flak too, because they're the players trying to shape the future.

The trade associations representing risk managers, producers and insurers have responded to their members' demands for assistance, support, direction, representation, and leadership. Association leaders encourage cooperative efforts when possible and from time to time select a technology solution and lobby for its use. But cooperation among competitors can be difficult and making technology decisions for others can discourage innovation.

The Change Conundrum

The conundrum of technological change is all around us. Take the development of the cashless society. Yes, we use plastic for many major purchases, but I'm tired of people writing checks and showing their driver's licenses to cashiers in long checkout lines. I'm tired of having to go to the ATM for cash to buy coffee or feed vending machines. I'm tired of emptying my pockets of change every night. The technology has been available to support a cashless society, but it too has been elusive... that is, until now.

We now have plastic cards containing chips that can draw money from either an ATM or a PC connected to a modem, as well as being used by swiping the card through a simple reader. The reading device reduces the balance on the card and uploads the amount to the vendor's account. These smartcard systems are in operation widely in Europe and Asia. French bank card users can slot their cards into their cell phone and download cash or make purchases.

One of the reasons why smartcard solutions in countries like France, Belgium and the Netherlands have been successful is they have gotten beyond the chicken-and-egg problem. The sponsoring industries have primed the pump with devices and media, rather than waiting for one player to make the first move.

In our industry, the chicken-and-egg problem remains with EDI (electronic data interchange) between agencies and insurers and with other forms of ebusiness transaction. Agencies will invest in the technology if enough insurers they represent can do business electronically, and insurers will invest in technology providing they can reach a critical mass of agencies selling their products.

Meanwhile in Europe, the Belgian government required the major banks to adopt the smartcard system. They took every opportunity to re-engineer devices to accept the smartcards, so they can be used directly in parking meters, mass transit gates, tollbooths and stores.

Retail banking's leadership in realizing the cashless society makes agency-insurer EDI pale by comparison. But the "pick a solution and get everyone to use it" approach may ultimately fail. In the first place, not all industries can agree on a single compelling cost saving that will underwrite the cost of wholesale change. In the case of banking, the cost of managing physical cash is enormous – and it cannot be handed on to the customer. How would you like to be charged a cent on every dollar you transacted in order to cover the costs of its secure movement around the cash system?

According to *The Economist* magazine, such a policy also "has a downside in that it can stifle change and retard further innovation." France's Minitel computer system was subsidized by the government and purchased by millions of families. Minitel is a kind of electronic telephone directory packaged with service offerings. According to *The Economist*, "those inflexible Minitel terminals are still in use a decade later, while the rest of the world has embraced the advantages of the Internet. France, once a leader, now lags behind."

Leaders Will Displace Competitors

All things being equal, market leaders who deliver the best solutions will displace others who do not. Trade associations are working to provide information on technology to their members either directly or through organizations like ACORD. They have formed committees and task forces to address policies and programs affected by technology. They are writing position papers, lobbying trading partners, fostering cooperative programs, and actively engaging in support of standards to make electronic commerce a reality.

When you consider how far we've come as an industry during such turbulent times, you will conclude that progressive association executives and volunteer leaders have responded well over the course of the past decade. The industry is working together to negotiate business and technology change. The best leadership is focused on interoperability, and the flexibility to innovate within common frameworks. Every day, technology brings us closer to this goal.

■

10

Data Duplication

Negotiating the invisible threats of data

In this chapter I bring the story of standards right back to insurance basics, with a discussion of how the industry has pursued reduction in information management efforts—and learned to eradicate the icebergs in its path.

The topic of this chapter is data duplication. In this simple phrase lies the nemesis of all the positive forces we examine in this book. The power to connect up business partners, the ability to manage our information infrastructure as a layer of services to the business, the use of common standards as a springboard to innovation and business enhancement... All these good things and more can all be nullified by the dread phrase "data duplication." Let your data proliferate, or demand your business information be entered into systems more than once, and the promise of the connected world crumbles to dust.

And if there's any doubt in your mind, be reassured that meeting an iceberg is not an outcome you want for your business journey. Just recall what the producers of 1970s disaster movie *Raise The Titanic!* said about the picture: "Raise the Titanic? It would have been cheaper to lower the Atlantic."

Enter Here

Duplicated data is not just a problem for the insurance industry. It is a problem for *every* industry. It's a fundamental business issue that challenges people the world over.

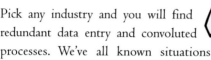

Pick any industry and you will find redundant data entry and convoluted processes. We've all known situations where people re-key information needlessly. When I find a customer services representative rekeying information for me, I'll make a sympathetic comment. They'll usually shrug or smile — and say the company is working on it.

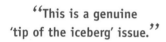

"This is a genuine 'tip of the iceberg' issue." This is a genuine "tip of the iceberg" issue. And most of us don't see or want to think about what lies beneath the surface.

In the insurance industry, the duplicated data issue goes by the name of "single entry." Single entry is what we'd like, but commonly don't have. It has been estimated 70 percent of all computer input is output from another computer system.

Have you ever wondered why the airline ticket agent seems to be writing a novel as you patiently wait for a flight change at the airport? Or why you can withdraw $250 from a cash machine with a plastic card, but not check into a $250-per-night hotel without going through a redundant check-in process? And if you want a really big iceberg, consider that almost one-half of the cost of our healthcare system is the result of "administrative overhead"— a euphemism for pushing paper and doing the same work over and over again. The single entry problem is everywhere.

But some companies are getting noticeably smarter. Several car rental companies offer special privileges to frequent renters. You complete an extensive application when you join the service, giving your driver's license number, credit card number, car preferences and so on. However, you never need to submit this information again. You make a reservation, providing travel dates and arrival time. At your destination, you board a bus at the curb, the driver asks your name, enters it into a computer, and drops you off in front of your car, trunk open. Upon your return, they scan the bar code in the windshield, the agent says "Welcome back, Mr. Smith," and prints your final receipt from a printer strapped around the attendant's waist. It works, it's a great service — and it's single entry.

Businesses today are awash with information. The amount of information is growing daily, as is the need to share information with our partners and customers. Single entry looms large on the business agenda and more and more decision-makers — from functions throughout organizations — are becoming sensitive to its significance.

Data 2 Go

Unlike the typical business transaction, insurance transactions are not light and simple. They carry a lot of freight. And the deeper you look, the more redundancy you find throughout the process.

This is one reason why many ACORD members are pursuing single entry as an overall strategy. They need to break down the silos of information within their own organizations. They need to understand what data they're using, and what they're using it for. And these aren't just issues for the agency distribution channel.

ACORD is known today foremost for its contribution to electronic standards. But ACORD was originally organized to address the single entry issue in the paper document environment. Independent agencies set out to eliminate entering — by typing or writing in longhand — the same information on different insurance company documents. Some thirty years later, we now use ACORD forms and have eliminated hundreds of thousands of proprietary forms and all the associated expenses. In effect, we achieved a breed of single entry that remains in use today, including computer-generated ACORD forms.

As agencies began to deploy computers, the need for single entry became ever more important and the extent of redundant data entry became even more obvious. And the early systems were not as integrated as they are today. I recall having to enter the same information into various modules of the *same* packaged system.

Those early agency systems were designed with cement walls. Moving information from one module to another was difficult or impossible. I remember the day when one vendor advertised a startling new feature allowing agents to convert prospects to customers without having to re-enter the data. Today we'd see this function as a simple change of status on an existing record, but the haphazard nature of early systems made it a minor miracle.

Agents would laugh when we talked about double entry in those days. They typically entered data many times in various contact, prospecting, proposal, rating, policy, and billing systems, not to mention several insurer terminals planted somewhere in the office as well.

With the urging of the trade associations, the single entry problem became a major discussion topic at nearly every industry event. But expectations continued to tower far above the reality of what could be achieved in the early days of business systems. The technology itself was limiting and costly, while software vendors were undercapitalized. At the same time few agencies were properly equipped and reliable communications networks were just emerging. And above all many of the business processes in place throughout the industry were ruled by the logic of another age.

The challenges became even greater as companies began to look at sharing data across organizational boundaries.

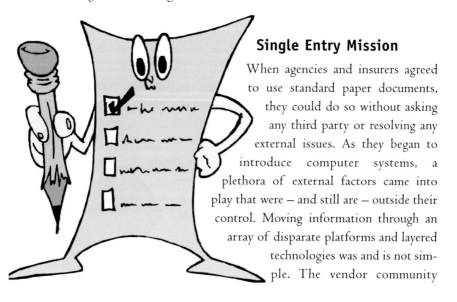

Single Entry Mission

When agencies and insurers agreed to use standard paper documents, they could do so without asking any third party or resolving any external issues. As they began to introduce computer systems, a plethora of external factors came into play that were — and still are — outside their control. Moving information through an array of disparate platforms and layered technologies was and is not simple. The vendor community (software, hardware and telecommunications providers) became major players in the pursuit of single entry. And the term SEMCI began to attract heavy attention.

SEMCI stands for "single-entry, multiple-company interface." The name has been in use for over twenty years now. It means, at its most basic level, the entry of data one time in a computer system. In other words, if a piece of information is already in a computer, all you ever need to do is to look it up, share it or transfer it. You do not want to enter it again, ever, regardless of the number of companies or software applications that use it. For independent agencies, SEMCI means entering insured application information once into their agency management systems for automatic transfer to insurers.

> **"You do not want to enter it again, ever."**

Single entry also means the entry of data one time for use in different insurer applications. Integrating data among underwriting, claims, billing, policy issuance, risk management and reinsurance systems is equally important. Data can be transferred to litigation or defense counsel assignment systems, property damage appraisal assignments, replacement rental systems, stolen vehicle tracking systems, rehabilitation assignment systems, and so on.

The "multiple company" ingredient of SEMCI is a key element, not only for independent agencies but for any business. Few organizations do business with a single trading partner. By trading partner I mean any party involved in a transaction: an agency, insurer, managing general agent, adjusting company, glass company, body shop, financial institution, policyholder, lienholder, or any other service provider. Business transactions typically involve exchanging information with hundreds and probably thousands of customers and other businesses. In effect, EDI now enables us to share information that is common to all trading partners and to increase everyone's productivity.

Most simple historical accounts of single entry are pessimistic. They miss all the subtleties involved in implementing single entry on a broad scale. Unfortunately, yet perhaps predictably, SEMCI has become viewed as a well-intentioned but foolhardy 1980s crusade, or a byword for failure.

The Problem is Systemic

The term SEMCI falls short of conveying the real meaning of information management in our connected world. Moving information was never "only" an agency-company issue. The problem is "systemic," meaning it affects the business as a whole, rather than one isolated part of it.

Ignoring the systemic nature of the problem results in bogus solutions that appease users in the short term but which offer no long-term return. A typical example is the transfer of redundancy from the agency to the insurer staff to give the illusion of a new and improved process.

Clearly, sweeping the iceberg under the rug isn't the way to solve the problem — even if it is a neighbor's rug. Exaggerated expectations and limited success with single entry solutions spawned widespread frustration and cynicism.

Some of single entry's bad press comes from confusion. Single entry gets confused with the technology used to achieve it. We get snarled in discussions about real-time processing versus batch-store-forward processing. We also talk about the merits of duplicating data at various locations or sharing it from a single location.

These are all valid technical debates. But the basic, simple and inescapable fact is we all want to avoid doing work twice. The critics fail to recognize the single entry issue is an underlying business trend or movement that continues to play out in the marketplace. Single entry cannot be viewed as a standalone project with milestones and target dates. It is not simply a matter of calling a meeting and agreeing to ban all redundant work in all business transactions.

> **"The pursuit of single entry is common across all industries."**

The pursuit of single entry is common across all industries. The movement lies behind Amazon's One-Click service, the Hertz Gold Club and e-tickets of all kinds. And it is also the raison d'être for all standards bodies in all industries. In the insurance industry, ACORD's Life Standards eliminate redundant data entry between life agency software products. ACORD EDI standards in Non-Life (Property and Casualty) do not eliminate all redundancies, but are widely used and credited with saving untold countless keystrokes.

Although it is a long-term, frustrating and often elusive goal, SEMCI is even more important in a world where all computers are being connected. Whether it's the big computer you drive (your car), the small one in your pocket (your cell phone or PDA), ever-smarter household appliances, or the networks that allow you to run a business, the key is they must share information in some way. The flow of information is the lifeblood of modern business.

Smoke Stacks & Stovepipes

Single entry has long been considered the ideal in a distribution system replete with isolated systems on desktops and within the enterprise. But today single entry is an essential business requirement. Competitive pressures simply don't allow us the luxury of inefficiency.

We may not be able to eliminate all the separate "stovepipe" systems in our business, but we now have the middleware tools to link and connect disparate systems that were not available to us in the past. So, though we may not want to integrate all our systems, we *can* make them collaborate. SEMCI, in native mode, means users do not have to repeat work by re-keying the same information in different computer systems. Of course, the corollary of not repeating work is the ability to exchange information with other computer systems.

Although this process of sending and receiving data has been referred to as "interface" in our industry, it is more accurately described as electronic data interchange (EDI). I would also include documents as part of the

"D" in EDI because we need to move and share unstructured data, like email and images, just as much as structured data. Structured data can be organized efficiently in databases and used readily by programs, whereas unstructured data only makes sense when looked at by a human user.

The original premise of the SEMCI model was the agency computer system would be the means of entering and storing information, and the exchange would be transparent to the end user. Exchange would be a byproduct of using the agency system.

We have had considerable success with EDI using standards, and the future continues to look bright. This is not only because agency systems are improving, but also because more niche vendor products are arriving to provide connectivity and add functionality not built in to traditional agency systems.

But why is the agency system seen as the primary vehicle for SEMCI and EDI? There are two drivers at work here. First, users wanted a consistent user interface. They didn't want to learn new screen layouts and commands for each business function they used. Second, users wanted to push the details and nuances of EDI into the background. Users shouldn't need to think about low-level issues relating to formats and communications. With these two aims met, the agency system would be the single gateway for communicating with trading partners.

The single-gateway model has had some success. Although agency systems have not grown to be all-inclusive portals, they now incorporate or connect with other software products and tools to get the EDI job done. Let's remember the original gateway models were responding to the growing number of insurer systems being placed in agencies to gather data for quoting and issuing policies.

One of the flaws of a single gateway model is the system must not only collect all information for all parties, but also deal with all changes. Even with standards in place, the differences among insurance products, the business rules and the edits used by insurers make the process extremely complex, particularly for commercial lines and life products.

Although the market has produced a number of middleware vendors and products providing such add-on EDI services, not all insurers are pleased with the result. So rather than defer data gathering and management to agency systems, some insurers prefer to gather information by using insurer host-driven systems.

It is unlikely that future of data collection will be based on a single gateway model. It seems like agencies will enter information into different systems for different purposes. The agency system might be the hub or primary system, but data will reside in or be used in other specialized systems. Insurers are increasingly using browser-based systems in the agency, using the Internet.

I spoke with a number of agents about the universal user interface in contrast to using insurer browser and other agency systems. Their overriding concern was with the workload and not as much with the learning curve. People can learn to use new and different tools, but it never makes sense to ask people to do the same work over and over again.

The key to preserving the goals of SEMCI is to ensure all these systems can share information. We must also ensure the information can move to all trading partners in the market.

"Ensure all these systems can share information."

Bit By Bit

The breakneck speed of technology advancement hasn't been slowed by the bursting of the dotcom bubble. The hype may have gone out of the market, but the IT industry just can't help innovating. Hardware continues to get smaller, lighter and faster. Software continues to get more robust and user friendly. Automation vendors are constantly offering new and improved products.

Technology is ubiquitous in our daily lives, but there is a wide gap between innovation and implementation. As in a clutch between a car's engine and its wheels, there is slippage. But compared to the past, we're doing quite well. For example, the typewriter was first described by a British inventor in 1714, but the first true working model, developed by the American inventor Christopher Sholes, did not appear until 1867. That's 153 years of lost keystrokes!

The principles of artificial refrigeration were discovered in 1748 in Scotland, but the first commercial home refrigerator was produced in 1913 and retailed for $900. There are few openings these days for icemen.

Today, change occurs rapidly and we implement technology closer to its point of innovation, but the gap remains. Improvement is a constant process, delivering small but incremental benefits. Our systems evolve. Improvement isn't a one-time goal: it's a way of life.

On the personal level, compare what you do with software to what it is capable of doing. Chances are you don't fully exploit the features of the product. On the grand scale, compare the level of automation in our business to what you know is available. We can always do more, and we will always find ourselves in this situation because technology changes faster than the people who use it.

One obvious reason for the innovation-implementation gap is few managers want to be the first to spend money on something new. They would rather be fast followers than first movers. Managers must contend with the established corporate culture and motivate employees to continuously climb a learning curve. The large organization struggles with massive inertia and legacy systems. The small organization needs to avoid going out of business as it reengineers the business. There will always be companies and agencies on the leading edge and some on the trailing edge, but most will be somewhere in the middle.

The acid test of whether you are using a database correctly is whether you have to use the paper files. A customer service representative should be able to handle inquiries and process transactions by looking at her screen and without referring elsewhere. If you can identify the implementation gap on your desktop and in your organization, you can also appreciate the size of the gap when you consider the industry as a whole. Most businesses maintain islands of automation by purchasing different software for different purposes, and most of the software does not exchange information. Consequently, double or triple entry of the same data at different times remains rife.

Diversity Magnifies Redundancy

For independent agencies, the diversity of companies' electronic interfaces magnifies the redundant data entry problem and reinforces the need for standards-based industry solutions.

The gap between innovation and implementation is closing as players begin to count the cost of inefficient processes and exclusion from the wider community. More managers are coming to realize the importance of planning proactively for technology implementation rather than reacting to vendor announcements or user request forms. Effective plan-

Peter Senge, author and consultant, asserts there is no such thing as a sustainable competitive advantage these days, other than our ability to learn. I often tell people technology is really not a matter of competitive advantage, but a matter of remaining competitive. New technologies will not only allow you to focus on the business: your continued success will demand you do.

Above The Icebergs

In the days of the great ocean-going liners, icebergs presented very clear and present dangers to shipping. As the *Titanic* went down, someone somewhere was working hard on a methodology for detecting icebergs, while others were laboring to devise new ways of clearing them from the shipping lanes.

By the late 1930s, we had found a new solution to the iceberg problem. It was called air travel.

We used a new technology to soar over the icebergs. We realized our problem was safe transportation, not iceberg management.

I believe the SEMCI issue has given way gracefully to a revitalized understanding of the underlying challenges of information flow in an increasingly connected business environment. That's where our energies are focused today.

---

70 percent of all computer input is output from another computer system.

- Once a piece of information is in a computer, all you should ever need to do is to look it up, share it or transfer it.

- SEMCI is not about technology, but about workflow.

- Technology is really not a matter of competitive advantage, but a matter of remaining competitive.

- If the world around you is conducting day-to-day business electronically and your business is not, you're going to lose.

11

The Fog of IT

Analyzing the fog of IT

Using IT in the organization is really difficult. Everyone knows that. Or do they? It strikes me the best performing executives I meet have a clear-headed and relaxed, capable style of leveraging and managing IT in their organizations. They're not blind to the risks that accompany any deployment of technology, but neither are they fumbling around in the dark as their competitors do.

Why do some organizations — the smart ones, the winners — get their arms around IT while others suffocate in technology's grasp? We're all dealing with the same quantities, so we all ought to be succeeding — or suffering — equally.

The simple answer is there's a kind of fog that gathers and settles around IT matters. The fog is always threatening to move in and engulf us. But some organizations choose to confront and dissipate the fog, while others accept the fog and the constraints it imposes on their business journey.

The aim of this chapter is to analyze the fog, and to begin to burn it off. You'll find that the fog of IT — the mix of uneasiness, distrust and doom that tends to stick to systems endeavors — settles in the minds of your colleagues unless you combat it. The fog is made up of ill-informed and half-formed beliefs that are rarely put into words. And because these vague feelings are not articulated, they are never challenged.

So, in this chapter I state the seven "Fog Factors" that produce the bulk of the world's IT fog. If the Fog Factors look a little crude and shocking, then I'm afraid that's what this kind of thinking looks like when you sum it up.

In the next chapter, I'll give you some specific tools for dispelling the fog of IT for all time. But first let's look at the seven Fog Factors, and see if they ring any bells for you.

Fog Factor 1

I need IT, but I don't need to love it, or even trust it. I keep that stuff in the basement, and I pay through the nose to keep it all running, so it can keep my business on its feet. I don't want to hear any more about it, unless you want to tell me it's getting cheaper, and then I won't believe you.

Is IT a necessary evil? An untrustworthy ally that needs houseroom but not affection? It seems IT in many organizations is a battleground: an arena of constant conflict and struggle.

And as a result we've bred a generation of IT para-managers. These are folks who are never happier than when they're fighting a big fire or launching a big systems rescue mission. There's usually an accompanying culture of all-nighters, demanded by a project planning approach that habitually underestimates resources and creates a vicious cycle of panic and pressure.

But IT today is not about heroics. It's about solid delivery. The wild frontier has been largely tamed. New commercial territories are opened up by advances in technology, but the business systems that follow the pioneer applications rely for 99 percent of their composition on existing know-how.

Incidentally, there are few real "paradigm shifts" in IT. And here's the skinny on those paradigm shifts that genuinely represent major advances: The shift is in the way we exploit technology, the way we think about it and use it. A paradigm shift is a new worldview, but not a new world. It doesn't mean that we throw away everything we have around us, but that we begin to exploit our environment differently. There was a time when the oil seeping out of the ground in Texas was cursed as a cattle poison, but the automobile created a paradigm shift that enabled us to exploit that oil.

> **"There are few real 'paradigm shifts' in IT."**

IT *is* integral to your business. And that means you should pay it *more* attention, not less. IT is a corporate health issue. And it's not just about keeping the body going, but making the body stronger and more agile too. To extend the metaphor, absorbing new developments in technology helps us develop new organs and limbs. IT can be an engine of business evolution.

Simultaneously, you should be *lowering* your estimation of IT. If your information capability really is there to keep the lights on reliably, then it should be treatable as a utility. It should need neither cursing nor nursing. The main reason IT installations frequently need constant care is they haven't been modernized. Systems are formed of patches and workarounds, and have evolved over several generations of platform and design approach. There's often little will to tidy up these anomalies, and an accompanying fear that touching any part of the systems edifice will bring it all crashing down. Yet unless issues of legacy systems are tackled, the enterprise will continue to carry unnecessary expense — and risk — in this area.

So, IT is important, but not glamorous. You need to give IT attention for the competitive advantage it can create for your organization, but also set reasonable expectations for mainstream service. Just because IT can create immense advantage for your business, that doesn't mean IT should play by rules any different than those that apply in other domains.

It's the same with people. People are hugely important to the enterprise, and they deserve respect and personal attention. But people are also "human resources" who must be managed, developed and deployed. We take these two complementary aspects for granted, just as we combine love and discipline in the nurturing of our children.

Extend the same principles to IT, and the world will get a little less foggy. Improve your IT capability so you can take its utility aspect for granted, and pay careful attention to the additional possibilities that IT offers. What we seek here is not a paradigm shift, but an attention shift. By all means keep your IT capability in the basement. But put some lights down there; and remember not to lock the door.

Fog Factor 2

CIOs and CEOs turn over even faster than major software releases. There's no time to implement any big changes in the way we do things, and even if there was, the folks who did the work wouldn't be around to reap the rewards.

It's true that visiting hours at the top levels of our organizations have shrunk. CxOs are unlikely to remain in place over decades, and some spend less than two years in a role before moving on.

But to assume that leaders only achieve trivial things while in position is unfair and inaccurate. Changes in the way IT is deployed in an organization may take time to roll out, but the strategic decision-making and leadership that inspires those changes can be summoned up and applied almost instantaneously.

It is also worth remembering that any investment made anywhere in the business by anyone is done for the sake of the business as a whole, and therefore all its stakeholders. The CxO's responsibility is to the business, not her own glory.

Having said that, there are a few strategic changes that CIOs can make which will also have the happy effect of making them superstars; and adopting standards is the chief of these.

CIO Superstar Strategies

• Adopt standards for business interoperability.
• Develop a services-based technical architecture for delivery.
• Build knowledge capital to enhance corporate book value.

Standards can be a big winner for the leaders who introduce them. Standards establish your credentials on the business side of the table; they show you are concerned both with recurring bottom-line savings and expansion of the business's trading potential; and they let you introduce a business language for talking about business processes, so you're no longer sidelined for talking in terms of system solutions.

Coming back to the short duration of most CxO appointments: Perhaps it's their short-term behavior that's driving their short-term placement? Many senior executives live and die at the whims of the market, now buoyed and now abandoned by sentiment that has little to do with the performance of their own companies. CIOs can find themselves attaching their fortunes to similarly ungovernable forces, particularly technology fashions. For example, many CIOs made large bets on the technology platform of choice for the future, only to find that the movement towards XML and web services has changed the decision factors. The result is a mass of companies with expensive but unused kit and licenses – and new CIOs. Successful CIOs don't bet. They take rational decisions, which they can articulate to the business. We'll have more to say on the CIO's role in the next chapter, when we look in more detail at dispelling the IT fog.

Fog Factor 3

IT is a battleground between technology nerds who love obscurity for its own sake and have no interest in our business and us, the business people who have to continually watch our bottom line and keep our customers happy. They're aided and abetted by vendors who want to sell us stuff we don't need. We're held to ransom by all these people because systems are complex and impossible to understand unless you're a specialist. The business is probably being ripped off royally, but then so is every other business, so it probably all works out.

This foggy thought results from a divergence between the thought processes, culture and goals of those who are "in the business" and those who are "in IT." Of course, *everyone* in the organization is in the business. IT specialists rarely see themselves as separate from the business, any more than people from other specialties do. We don't label our legal people or our finance people as nerds. (Well, maybe we do.) We try to respect the different contributions different specialties bring to the mix, and to manage our professional diversity.

Some members of the IT community have indeed provided the models for this Fog Factor. But the growing professionalism of the community is tending to isolate such individuals. The majority of IT folks in business today are just as dedicated to, and motivated by, the enterprise's corporate goals as their colleagues in other disciplines.

The *apparent* disconnect between IT and non-IT people is due to a crucial communications gap, as we saw in *Chapter 8: The Digital Divide.*

Fog Factor 4

IT projects are inherently uncontrollable. They're big, messy and complex, so it's no surprise that no one can keep them on course. It's better to do little projects, and it's best to do no projects. We haven't earned out our investment so far, so why should we spend any more?

Fog Factor 4 represents a heartfelt reaction to the challenge of managing the IT mission. I've been in IT for as long as IT has existed, and I appreciate that this stuff can be hard to get right. But I don't believe there's anything inherently <u>un</u>controllable about IT. In fact, I think IT is, if anything, inherently controllable. IT is a great deal easier to manage, measure and modify than is, for example, marketing.

Managing any complex endeavor is a challenge. But IT is a mature profession, and the profession has built up an impressive mass of tools, techniques, patterns, methodologies and architectures that embody the best practices of those generations of men and women who have built and deployed great business systems. Standards are a key component of that professional heritage — available to all, irrelevant to none.

However, it is true that IT projects do sometimes fail, but no more or less than projects in any other domain. There is nothing special that applies only to IT and not to marketing, or product development, or operations, or logistics — or, for that matter, catering.

We looked at why IT projects fail — and how you can stop them from failing — in Chapter 4.

Fog Factor 5

The speed of technology change is bewildering. They're always bringing out something new, and claiming it's the last word. I've seen so many "killer applications" I'll kill the next person who uses the phrase. We need to get our arms round the IT we have, and not think about changing anything.

Stop the world, I want to get off! This Fog Factor arises from a disconnect between the speed with which people can envision a technology, and the time it takes to realize that technology's benefits in the real world. We'll have more to say on the nature of this disconnect, where we relate the potential of technology to the reality of business achievement.

The fact is, the much-quoted "bewildering rate of change" is overplayed. It makes for a good excuse for not taking rational decisions about technology. But letting your organization stand frozen in the headlights of the latest technology bandwagon is no more constructive than clambering aboard without asking where it's headed. If you believe you can't cope with change, then you'll condemn the enterprise to treading water — generating a lot of froth, but no forward motion, and no (financial) returns.

Fog Factor 6

Our system requirements are unique. They must be, because our business is like no other. And that's how we stay ahead. We grow all our own timber, and we don't need any lessons from other players. What do you want us to do — copy something that wouldn't work as well?

Some percentage of what you do is unique. A larger percentage is common to all your competitors. Unless you enjoy a monopoly over some line of business, then you must play by rules that are common to your industry. If you don't, your customers won't recognize you as a supplier or understand your offer when you confront them.

We could debate where the split comes between common and unique attributes in the insurance industry, but in reality the exact ratio differs from player to player. Also, the value of the smaller "unique" element should overwhelm the apparent value of the common element, making it harder to assess where the split lies. So, for example, a firm might concentrate on excellent customer service by investing in personal account managers for high-value customers. The company's products could be entirely generic, and functionally indistinguishable from a thousand other suppliers. Yet the customer service layer creates immense competitive advantage, and distinguishes the player in the market.

Differentiation is a vital value-add for businesses, but it is an "add." We differentiate by adding a twist to a trusted formula. The twist should be valuable enough — in the customer's eyes — to overwhelm the vanilla nature of the rest of the enterprise's functions. But we, as leaders of that enterprise, should not be working to the same logic. What makes us different makes us strong. But what makes us similar gives us life.

Recognize where your unique/common split occurs, and invest accordingly. You'll need to invent processes, techniques and maybe even products and services to support your unique element. This is where you accomplish what only you can accomplish: where you create your organization's standout features. It may be that no one else can teach you here, though it's just as likely you will learn much from non-competing industries or other knowledge domains.

But don't let your common area go without attention. The common area will always account for the larger proportion of an enterprise's functionality. If you ignore it, it will sicken and fail. If, on the other hand, you mistake it for an extension of your unique area, you will spend too much on inventing processes and systems that do not contribute to your competitive edge. You've heard about "not re-inventing the wheel." Well, your common area encompasses the wheels, engine, and floor plan of your business. The unique part of your business is the way you organize the internal space: it's where the people go. In other words, it's not about the process or the data but rather it's about competing on the business rules.

Misunderstanding your organization's uniqueness can lead to several corporate health problems. Organizations that focus on the functions that differentiate them are like people who join a gym to train on weights, but forget to eat. Organizations that think all their attributes are unique remember to eat, but insist on inventing every recipe from scratch, growing all their own ingredients, never go out to a restaurant, and never have anyone over. It's amazing they get anything else done!

Fog Factor 7

We're doing as well — or as badly — with our IT as everyone else. Every other company is in the same boat, in the same fog. So, since we're all equal, there's no point in our trying to do better with IT. We need to wait for the whole industry to improve, then we'll benefit from that. The tide will come in, and raise all the boats.

This is the most comforting illusion of all: that everyone is in a state of confusion, without direction and without advantage. Those ships you sense passing yours in the night — they're not headed anywhere either.

How wrong. For every subscriber to the fog theory of IT, there's a competitor for whom the fog no longer exists. They have driven away the fog with rational thinking. They have brightened the gloom by adopting sound management practices. They have learned to value IT correctly, and to deploy it with devastating effect. And wherever you think you're going — well, they're going to get there first.

It's easy to get stuck with the wrong solutions when you're in the fog!

I know I've drawn some caricatures in this analysis of the IT fog. But I challenge you not to find these unvoiced thoughts in the minds of colleagues you have known, or competitors you have met. The chances are your own continued success derives from the methods you have discovered to dispel the fog, and to keep if from returning. In the next chapter, I cover the main ways that successful businesses have dealt with the fog, and emerged into the light.

12

Beacons In The Fog

Getting into the IT AREA

How can we burn away the fog, and rediscover the real mission of IT? We need to get back on track, hold fast to the goals that matter, and make confident progress.

I have four keys to offer you. They will help you maintain a clear focus on value amid the fog of IT.

These keys make up the acronym AREA, and they are:
• Articulate IT's contribution
• Risk Of Not Investing (RONI)
• E-business is just business
• Achieve 10x with 1/10
Let's look at the keys one by one.

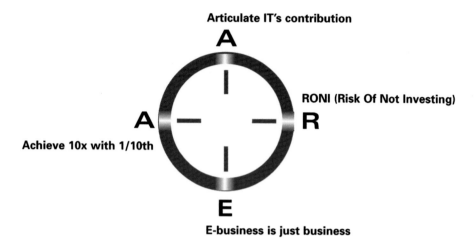

Fig 10: Covering the Area

Articulate IT's Contribution

One of the clearest messages to emerge from my discussions with CIOs and other key decision-makers in today's organizations is the CIO's urgent role as an articulator. The CIO's prime value to the organization, her unique contribution, is her ability to understand and communicate why, how and where the organization is spending on information technology. Make no mistake: IT makes up a gigantic – and growing – proportion of any enterprise's spend. And the other CxOs don't have the skills, experience – or responsibility – to make the IT story stand up.

> **"The savvy CIO uses four keys to maintain a clear focus on value amid the fog of IT."**

Gary Beach, editor of *CIO Magazine*, told ACORD's 2003 Conference technology accounts for 50 percent of an organization's capital expenditure. By 2010, that figure will be 70 percent. The figures come from Morgan Stanley, and they apply to all industry sectors.

IT is a young profession, and many of our leaders can still remember when "data processing" was a pocket fiefdom of the finance department. In its youth, IT was designed to address internal integration, in a self-contained environment. The proprietary, hardwired solutions that were developed back then, however, are ineffective in today's networked world. In the forty or so years IT has been hatching, growing and (sometimes) rampaging throughout our organizations, it has never quite managed to shake off the trappings of the adolescent. We've given IT plenty of slack. When it's disappointed us, we've told ourselves "it's just a phase."

No longer. IT is subject to the same rigors as every other business discipline. We expect IT leaders to be numerate, business-savvy communicators. We measure their performance by business criteria. We insist on rational and rounded procurement, development and acceptance processes. And we have seen the IT industry evolve towards commoditized software, outsourced services, downsized development teams.

"And we have seen the IT industry evolve towards commoditized software, outsourced services, downsized development teams."

Now the IT function has grown up, CIOs need to understand the corporate spotlight shines on them 24/7. CIOs must not wait to be asked for their assessment of IT's contribution to the business. They need the numbers, and the context and assumptions that go along with those numbers, at their fingertips.

When we use the word *articulate*, we think of people speaking clearly and instructively, so their message is communicated faithfully to their audience. But "articulated" also means something has "clearly distinguishable parts." When we articulate something, be it a model or a message, we create an object from linked parts.

So, articulating IT's function in the contemporary organization isn't just about saying what's going on in the development teams, or reporting what the *wider* IT community believes to be the key issues of the technology landscape. Articulating the IT function is about assembling an argument other folks can follow. It's about constructing a legible account of the decisions, actions and outcomes that have brought the organization to the place where it is today. And, for the CIO, articulating IT is also crucially about extending this chain of logic into the future, and accounting for the actions the organization is set to make in order to meet — and change — its future.

The CIO's role is therefore far from passive. CIOs have to be creative. The skills a CIO might have used earlier in her career to analyze a systems problem or design a systems solution need to be applied at a much higher level. This is a level beyond business analysis or information architecture — or whatever pinnacle you choose to identify at the top of the IT heap. It's a level of skill, creativity and commitment that truly sits above the formal content of any traditional description of any computing-based discipline.

This is big-table stuff. When I talk about articulating IT's function, I don't just mean the CIO's job is to answer questions about how much is being spent on what and why. I mean the CIO is engaged in a constant mission to discover and tag evidence; to construct chains of cause and effect; to describe and compare alternate courses of action, and choose amongst them in the best interests of the organization; to absorb the stream of announcements and claims from the IT industry and filter the viable from the friable.

Today's CIO needs to control and connect the key determinants of success in the information arena, and lay out the path she has chosen for the organization's IT so her peers can appreciate its contribution to the enterprise's mission.

CIO Skills

Once you have burned off the fog of IT, you will be able to see the landscape again. With the return of vision comes the responsibility to be a pathfinder, a road-layer, a highway-constructor. I think of successful CIOs as people who can scout a safe path toward an objective, select the right tools, people and tactics to lay a durable road, and go on to set up and direct the building of the Interstate that will take the majority swiftly and comfortably to the objective.

These functions are all — in the model-making sense — articulations. Put them together and you have a portrait of the mature CIO: someone who spans the range of behaviors from pioneer to maintainer. This breadth of skills, and the flexibility needed to apply the skills well, is a key clue to the success and longevity of professional CIOs.

Not all CIOs have the breadth and flexibility the role demands. Too much pioneer spirit, and you end up chasing new fads. Some of those fads may score the organization success in the market, but it's a risky approach. You may offset the risk of new technologies by using a portfolio approach to your IT investments. But if you never move on to the consolidation and maintenance phases, your systems infrastructure will be a rickety, make-do structure. Remember, the successors of the earliest airplane inventors built on the principles the pioneers exposed, not the piano wire they used to make their planes.

> "Offset the risk of new technologies by using a portfolio approach to your IT investments."

On the other hand, if a CIO is too focused on the maintenance phases of IT, then the organization is likely to spend too much of its resources on legacy systems, and avoid the potential benefits of new technology. I have heard senior IT folks explain that marshalling and managing legacy skills and systems is okay for their business, because they have always grown their own solutions and could never find any superior wisdom in the outside world.

I wonder if this was ever true; but I know for certain that in the connected world we now live in, arguments that rely on in-enterprise peculiarity no longer hold water. Sure, you may have the best ever automated process for handling a claim, or calculating a premium. But that has no value if it cannot be exposed to and used by your trading partners. And since customers now have easy access to alternate suppliers via ubiquitous connectivity, your customers can now rapidly decamp to another source.

In every sphere of life, uniqueness is always being challenged. IT used to be protected from some aspects of competition by the isolation of its systems, development languages, run-time platforms and accessibility routes. Standardization has torn down those walls.

The Elevator Pitch

Entrepreneurs and sales professionals talk about the "elevator pitch": the short, to-the-point summary of your business proposition you need always at the tip of your tongue. Successful CIOs use a cousin of the elevator pitch to ensure they're always in good shape to characterize their contribution: the *defensible position*. Think of the defensible position in battle-strategic terms. Your defensible position is your IT policy in a succinct form. It incorporates the challenges faced by the organization and the measures you have taken to meet those challenges. It's a position because it is defined in terms of an environment and a goal set; and it's defensible because you designed it that way. You don't always have to be on "the high ground." But you need to know where you stand, why you're there, and how to convey the strategic benefits of your position.

It may sound like I'm demanding a lot from CIOs. If so – good. Being an officer of a great human enterprise isn't meant to be easy, and the last time I looked the compensation was pretty reasonable. Most CIOs I meet embody the traits I've been discussing here. They articulate, and they operate across the range. To sum up their successful behavior, I'd say achievement as a CIO rests in the direction of attention. How you direct an organization involves directing people and directing investment: essentially, it's about facilitating the flow of resources to the right places. How you pick those places, communicate the locations to others, and make sure they arrive there intact, is down to the attention you pay to your environment, your goals and your resources. Taking the responsibility to articulate IT – in its fullest sense – is an excellent way of training your attention, and releasing your power to enhance the business.

Risk of Not Investing

We owe *CIO Magazine's* Gary Beach a further debt for his coining of the acronym RONI: Risk Of Not Investing. He echoed Larry Downes, our keynote speaker at ACORD's 2003 Conference, by showing how downtimes in the economic cycle are prime times for investment. Gary extended the concept to suggest that while the downturn is an excellent time to invest, upswings in the cycle need to be accompanied by IT investment as well.

There's no standing still in IT, if there ever was. The difference today is mature organizations control the agenda for change. They don't let vendors or the media determine where or when their investments will be made. They make their own decisions about making new investments, and about pulling investments in projects that aren't delivering on their promises. They know IT is no longer a matter of *whether* to invest, but a matter of *how* to invest. They are directors of resource, seeking to make the best decisions they can on behalf of the business's mission.

Short-term thinking has led to a focus on ROI (Return On Investment) cases as justifying mechanisms for IT projects. While we should applaud any support for rational management, we should not imagine organizations ever threw away the business case discipline, even during the headiest days of the Bubble era. Indeed, even in the most conspicuous cases of headlong e-spend amongst established enterprises, you don't have to look hard to find the edges of a supporting business case.

"Every CIO must construct future scenarios." The lineage of the typical large-company e-business investment can be traced to the need to support the company's share price during the bull market, and the perceived need to stake out online territory ahead of competitors or new entrants. These aims made perfect sense at the time the decisions were taken, and are to be distinguished from the gaseous business plans of those dotcom startups that were betting on being able to "monetize" non-paying customers at some distant date in the future.

In the great majority of enterprises, repetition of the primacy of ROI cases smacks of Egg-sucking 101. They never did sign away big budgets on projects that didn't target an identifiable and measurable business win. But the ROI mantra is likely to enforce a degree of parochialism in the decisions they take in the post-Bubble era. ROI methodologies often entice planners to restrict their vision to the variables they can most easily measure, rather than the ones that might have most impact on the business. At the broadest level, it is always simpler to tackle a project that promises cost savings than it is to model a project that targets revenue growth. Revenue growth seems to demand faith, whereas cost cutting can be tracked to the accounts in milliseconds.

"On the other hand . . ."

The Risk Of Not Investing is the aggregated downside represented by a failure to look precisely at these less tractable metrics. No one can read the future. But every CIO can, and must, construct scenarios of how the future may turn out – and take the appropriate actions to safeguard the enterprise's health according to her judgment of the likelihood of each scenario's occurring, and its impact on the business, which has its origins in military strategy but much of its developmental history in the energy industry, does not shy away from long timelines, complex environmental interactions, or potential catastrophes. (Ring any bells? It sounds a lot like what the insurance industry has been doing for centuries.)

Working up scenarios, and working through them, can be time-consuming. But the practice also gives you incredible mastery over the future. By applying scenario planning, you can address the future before it happens. As life throws events at the business, you'll be able to draw from a growing pool of ready responses. It's almost like psyching out the future. Scenario planning is used mostly for preparing against disasters, where it is often given the more upbeat name of "business continuity." I believe we're all in the business of business continuity, so we should be modeling and meeting a range of predictable futures.

Learn, Assess, Test

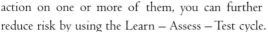

Scenario planning can help to manage your IT investments and reduce RONI. When you come to assess your business scenarios and decide to take pre-emptive action on one or more of them, you can further reduce risk by using the Learn – Assess – Test cycle.

Say you have articulated a scenario in which a powerful new market entrant decides to undercut prices in order to "buy the business" and raze the ground of existing providers. Your business response might be to switch from differentiation by price to a focus on service value-add. How can you add service to your product offering, and do so in such a way that it justifies a high premium? There may be a number of ways in which technology could help you achieve this goal, perhaps by allowing customers the convenience of anytime, anywhere self-management of their product, or perhaps by linking up with suppliers of complementary goods and services and creating an exclusive valued-added bundle. Figuring these options, and how you might implement them, is the learning phase.

As you learn about your options and potential implementations, you may revise your original scenario or narrow the range of viable ways forward. At this point, you are in the assessment phase. For the CIO, assessment often involves product demonstrations and trials as new pieces of software are put through their paces. But assessment should also extend to the effectiveness of solutions within the business context. In other words, we should be asking not just whether a particular solution works, but whether it works in our organization, and for our customers. We're measuring against business goals.

The pilot phase of the cycle lets us run small-scale projects to see if our initial assessment stands up to the rigors of real life. We pick an area of the business in which to apply the solution, and measure its performance against set goals.

Learn

Assess

Test

Can the cycle apply to the adoption of standards? Certainly, learning about and assessing standards is eminently doable. These actions should be a continually revisited part of any CIO's defensible position, whether or not her position is to use standards! If you are rejecting standards, know why you are doing so, and be prepared to state your logic. But can an organization really test or pilot standards? If standards are all-consuming and all-encompassing, then does using them in one part of the business teach us anything?

I believe that piloting standards does indeed make perfect – and vital – sense. Yes, standards should be applied everywhere. But they can be *proven* anywhere. I'd say the same thing for any pervasive technology, whether it was a power source, or a currency, or a management style. Reward and recognition schemes, for example, make little sense unless they are available to all staff members and integrate with the enterprise's business practices, ethics and leadership values. Yet such schemes can be readily piloted in areas of an enterprise, where the trials yield both intrinsic performance data and comparative performance data. It doesn't matter that the scheme has not been deployed in its entirety. Pilot projects have different fish to fry. They aim to expose weaknesses in the solution, to reveal how the solution should be tailored to the needs of the organization, and, not least, to suggest how the solution should be rolled out in its entirety.

The business-to-business features of ACORD's standards imply that if you're to get the most from them even in a pilot situation you need a trading partner to work with. Some users meet the chicken-and-egg problem here. How do parties get their systems to work with each other if their systems are not working with each other? Who makes the first move?

The ACORD community can provide collaborative parties for pilot projects. One of the benefits of our community nature is the ability to make connections amongst members and extend a helping hand across the organization's current boundary. No standards user need stand alone today.

E-business Is Just Business

The days when you were obligated to bolt the letter e- onto the front of other words to signify you were bringing connectivity to bear on some domain are long gone. IBM unveiled its "e-business" campaign in 1997, helping to raise the profile of Internet technologies as business enablers. E-business as a term is ready for the scrap heap. That doesn't mean it's failed. Far from it. The fact is, all business is now e-business. And that's the same as saying e-business is just business.

Information technology has become part of the DNA of every business. IT is not going to be purged from the corporate world. As the NASDAQ fell in the spring of 2000, you'd have been forgiven for assuming gangs of removers were touring the offices, factories, stores and homes of the world tearing out PCs and ripping up cables. What actually happened was a mass of hype vanished from the market. Unrealistic valuations of future events, and of future shares of future markets, were discounted. But this process had little, if anything, to do with how IT was being used in the real world.

E-business has been a great success. We now have online procurement through catalogs for common business goods and services, from stationery to travel. We can access business services such as payroll, HR management or CRM over the net. We can track inventory at our suppliers, as well as ongoing deliveries. We can open up our internal systems to trusted partners via extranets. Mobile devices enable us to

"E-business has been a great success. "

stream information to wherever it is needed in the organization. Connectivity allows us to outsource business processes globally. Every business today is an electronic business, whether it's a home-based mail-order business accepting orders via email or distributing its goods on E-bay, or whether it's a multinational corporation that synchronizes its supply chain through interworking, XML-talking systems.

The magic – the glamour, even – the PC and then the Internet brought to IT folks in enterprises has become part of everyday life. An employee with a PC at home will almost certainly have a machine of a higher specification at home than at work, if only because he will probably have bought it more recently, benefiting from steadily reducing prices and increasing functionality. The web has demystified the miracle of getting words and pictures to appear on a screen, since most people can knock out a home page without any special training or tools. Search engines such as Google have shown people the answer to almost any query they could imagine is reachable within a few seconds.

None of these advances turns ordinary Joes into genius software engineers. But the spread of computer literacy and net connectivity has indeed stripped the IT profession of much of its mystique. "If my son can put a page up with a picture of his dog on it, how come I can't get the latest sales figures?" There's any number of answers to this common question, but the only right one is: "You can."

Defending IT's mystique is a sure way to generate more fog. Focusing on the subtleties of technology implementation in the face of business demands is equivalent to pumping out noxious smoke to mingle with the existing fog. Face it: We got what we wanted. It's all IT now. And the job now is to make it work.

Achieve 10x With 1/10

The fourth and last element of our fog-dispersing strategy is the brightest beacon of them all. This is the stark commandment I hear at many leading businesses: Achieve 10x with 1/10. That's right: not only must you achieve ten times as much as you did yesterday, but you must do it with one tenth of the resources. And guess what? Once you've achieved that, you're going to have to achieve it again.

Step changes of this magnitude seem awesome. And yet we have achieved such miracles many times. Mechanization of all kinds has improved yields, quality and efficiency of resource usage over many cycles in agriculture and manufacturing. Whenever we are warned fossil fuels are in danger of running out, we find new ways to extract oil that was previously inaccessible, and new methods of using it in ever-more efficient engines and plants. There may be limits to human expansion, but those limits seem to recede every time we feel their approach.

The same advances occur in business. And each time we achieve a step change, we rapidly become accustomed to it, and forget the previous situation. Try to imagine modern business without the telephone. Coming closer to the experience of our own generation, try to imagine business without email. Email lets us communicate with many more people and much more cheaply than any previous form of written communication. The explosion in textual communications email has ignited brings its own problems; but these should not blind us to email's overwhelmingly positive impact on business productivity, reach and auditability.

> **"Try to imagine modern business without the telephone."**

It's always hard to foresee what the catalyst of the next step change will be. Part of the delight we all take in business is the way a new technology or business approach can rise out of left field and change the landscape for us all. From budget airlines to $4 lattes, business has a way of prompting double takes. "You can really fly from there to there for that much? But the coffee at the airport costs *how much*? And *no refills?*"

If you keep the step-change beacon brightly lit in your mind and in the concerns of your team, then you are more likely to make — or take advantage of — the catalyzing agent when it arises. Seeking this catalyst is a prime aspect of the CIO's responsibility. "Business as usual" is all very well, and, yes, we expect our IT people to "keep the lights on" and "keep the show on the road." But we also want our IT leaders to find us the business-as-usual of tomorrow: the extraordinary new world where we can do much, much more with much, much less.

How Standards Help To Dispel The IT Fog

Articulate IT's Contribution

Standards embody a language for describing businesses. A mature standard is an articulated model, designed to be exploited and challenged by human beings. Use standards as your articulation platform, and as a rich toolkit for developing your own unique account of where the business is headed.

RONI

Standards are a leveraged investment. Ninety percent of the investment needed to bring the benefits of standards to play in your organization exists within the fabric of the standards themselves. By adopting standards, you are acquiring the knowledge capital of your peers and partners. By applying the final ten percent of localized knowledge and deployment effort, you will reap the full reward. Ignoring standards is therefore one risk that is very easily calculated.

E-business Is Just Business

Standards create business interoperability. Without a common set of business definitions agreed by the interested parties, industries cannot communicate effectively and efficiently with each other. Standards such as ACORD's add a layer of business capability over the raw electronic transport mechanisms of Internet-based systems. With every player potentially connected to every other player, business standards ensure doing business across those connections is straightforward, cost-effective, reliable – and meaningful.

Achieve 10x With 1/10

Standards have a multiplier effect on productivity. Using standards gives you access to a massive range of potential customers and business partners, whilst massively reducing your cost of doing business with any and all of those parties. The organization does much more, with much less. Developers create systems faster, with compressed analysis and design phases and swifter passes through the vendor selection maze. Designers of new products and services can get more offers to market more quickly, and to wider markets. Standards represent the catalyst of a step change you can import cleanly to your organization today.

13

Mindset Matters

How you think determines how you perform

In this chapter we look at how a decision-maker's mindset determines the actions he takes, and therefore the success of his — and his organization's — mission. First, I question whether it's possible to have the commercial benefits of standards without adopting standards themselves. You won't be surprised to learn it can't be done. But it's worth rehearsing the reasons, since the hope enterprises will succeed without standards is often seductive. You need to know how to expose the falseness of this *hope* in order to save your organization from painful folly.

Second, I look briefly at the divergent mindsets of successful and unsuccessful CxOs. The divergence is largely down to how people orient themselves to the future and take responsibility for the way ahead.

Third, I examine how standards act as an invisible lubricant in business, ensuring the enterprise engine runs smoothly, safely, and economically. The purpose of this section is to highlight the serious consequences for corporate health of *not* adopting standards.

Finally, I look at the role of reason in running businesses, and explain how standards embody responsible, rational business leadership.

Business *Without* Standards

Can organizations and industries flourish without standards? Is there some other way the benefits of standards can be achieved – perhaps in an informal, self-determining manner?

It would be cool if the benefits standards bring could be discovered in the baggage of some other component of business. I believe people have tried to search for these free benefits, though they may not have known what they were doing was trying to find an alternative to standards. But this is the only way I can account for the faith some organizations have placed in several informal approaches to establishing business interoperability, information quality and process transparency – the effects standards such as ACORD's bring to business.

My observation is such organizations propose one or more of three distinct alternatives to standards. These are, if you will, informal containers of competence. They are:
• Experience
• Genius
• Justification

Experience

Experience is the growth hormone of individual and corporate wisdom. Without experience, we have no way of judging whether our actions have had the effects we desired of them. Experience gives us the right to rule on the actions of the less experienced, and gives us a rough-and-ready tool with which to judge novel situations.

But experience is worthless unless we learn from it. Experience that is not considered, consolidated and communicated to those who would benefit from it has no value. It may act as a status marker within the organization, but I hope we can agree such distinctions have no interest for us as business people.

The chief attribute of unmanaged experience is its suitability for flight. Experience leaves. It walks out of the building every evening, and sometimes it doesn't return. It isn't an asset you can confidently factor into your assessment of the business's powers.

The way humans learn from experience is to reflect upon it, seek patterns amongst it, and communicate it clearly to others. That's as good a definition of the standards-setting process as you'll find. One of the functions of standards is to capture experience, and turn it into knowledge capital. Standards bring usability and durability to experience.

Genius

The genius of a person or an organization – or of a place, one of the concept's earliest usages – is a kind of spirit. We use the concept of genius to externalize the random nature of inspiration and insight. It's a pleasing fiction that helps us retain a bit of magic in an otherwise rational world.

I'm not denying there are smart people, and less smart people. But when we rely on the leadership and innovations of those who seem particularly gifted, we can be cruelly misled. Genius is notoriously unreliable, and loading one or more individuals within an organization with the responsibility of being consistently smarter than everyone else is a good way to lose the plot. Think of the innovative funding vehicles at Enron, which few people could understand and fewer were willing to question.

Genius does indeed spark within organizations, in every department and every day. It's a distributed effect that happens when people work together: a kind of electricity generated by human interaction. The isolated genius rarely has a genuine role to play within modern organizations, except perhaps in a rarefied R&D role – and even here (especially here), commercial organizations are concentrating more and more on deliverability rather than novelty for its own sake.

Genius, like experience, has to be captured, examined and transformed into something that can affect the future actions of the organization. It is a source of raw power, not institutional guidance. And it's obvious where the fruits of genius should be set to ripen: within the standards-making process. This is the place where ideas can be tested against the basic, universal measures of business and the unique measures and meanings of the organization's specific business domain. Standards allow us to filter ideas and insights, matching them to scales of business practicality, probity and profit. They provide a conductor for the random lightning of genius, transforming genius from an untrustworthy sprite to a helpful power.

Justification

Justification is the process of interpreting past actions as optimum solutions, despite apparent evidence to the contrary. It's a way of fixing the parameters of a problem situation in retrospect, so the organization's behavior seems correct. We'll meet this effect in more detail shortly when we look at CxO mindsets, and how poor concentration on his responsibility to the future can blind a business leader to the transforming and enduring value of standards.

By justifying the situation we find ourselves in, we negate the need for standards because any mismatch between intention and outcome is magically "fixed." The organization appears to progress in a dreamlike state, performing haphazardly but always to plan. If you live inside such an organization, then it is all too easy to assume the enterprise has the key to success, and to believe it has nothing to learn from external organizations – or, in fact, from itself, since its own history is being constantly rewritten. A faultless performance needs no guidance.

> **"The organization's experience won't persist without standards."**

Clearly, justification is just irresponsible management with institutionalized cover-up thrown in. It may surprise you that organizations with such pathology don't readily swap their current dysfunctional behavior for the light and sense standards would bring them. After all, their justificatory behavior shows they're not scared of a little hard work; and adopting standards would be less work, and more useful.

But, by definition, justification is about self-delusion. Folks who are stuck in this situation can rarely see an alternate way of life – until they are brutally shown by a competitor.

Back To Earth

Questions are a good way of bringing organizations back from states of self-delusion, and turning up the focus on business necessities. The key questions any enterprise needs to ask of itself are these:

1. How do we connect with our customers?

2. Where is our information coming from?

3. Can we bring it into our systems efficiently?

4. How can we share it with trading partners?

5. How do we pass it to others who need it?

6. How do we connect our corporate systems to literally thousands of computers around the world, including the consumer's desktop?

7. Are we going to need to translate every piece of information that comes into or goes out of our firm?

8. How do standards lower our costs?

9. What are the dangers of proprietary systems?

10. What standards affect what parts of our organization?

11. How do business changes and regulators' mandates translate into revised standards?

12. Is there any single person in this organization who knows about all the standards that we need, and the actions we need to take?

Ad-Hoc-ism

The common thread amongst these counter-standards is their sanctioning of ad-hoc actions. Each assumes businesses can run successfully without some means of expressing and making persistent the processes, data and relationships that form the business. Each assumes that transactions, both inside and outside the organizational boundary, require no governance, no common support, no corporate accountability. Smart people, using their hard-won experience, try to do their best and if things don't work out, well, there will be a whole list of reasons why they really *did* work out. The organization's experience won't persist without standards: the best it can hope for is experience will be imitated, and that it will be imitated faithfully and in relevant situations.

The organization's genius will have no accountability: in the best situations, genius may be endorsed by someone higher up the chain of command, which is one way of hiding the problem. And the organization's justified history will ensure it has no auditability: it will be impossible to judge the actions of the enterprise, or to value the business, or to assess its continuing viability.

These are the implications of ad-hoc business. Acting on the spur of the moment, without reference to a model of how the business should work, creates a fragmented, discontinuous business: one that does not know itself. These behaviors also isolate the enterprise in its peer group and its industry. By avoiding standards, the organization denies itself markets, partners and growth opportunities.

Switching Mindsets

How leaders behave depends on their default thought patterns. Human cognition is obviously a complex area to start delving in, and I don't want to be accused of overturning the cliché that "this isn't brain surgery." But in crude terms, it's clear successful leaders are easily distinguished by their *ownership of the future*. The two following models explain what I mean.

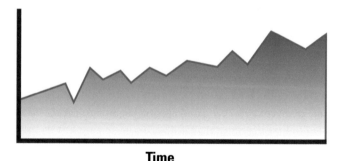

Time

Fig 12: Standard Historical View of Performance

The Wrong Mindset

Someone with this mindset:
- Expects to be judged on past performance alone.
- Measures his own business against current and historic competition only.
- Believes his performance to date justifies his current attitude to the future.
- Sticks to proven formulas.

The Right Mindset

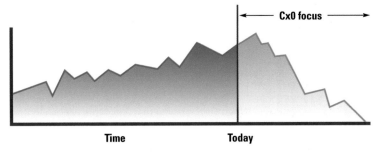

Fig 12.2: CxO Focus on the Future

Someone with this mindset:

- Is able to construct scenarios of the future.
- Has an objective view of potential risks and disruptions.
- Learns from the past but integrates other information into the decision-making process.
- Focuses on shaping the future, not reshaping the past.
- Challenges received wisdom.
- Exploits tools and techniques developed in his environment.

Mindset And Standards

- Leaders have a responsibility to manage the future, not justify the past.
- Effective leaders project their businesses into the future, and examine a range of scenarios that might apply in their environment.
- Common factors in the future of all industries include greater interconnection, competition and responsiveness.
- Standards address these factors head-on and will maintain and improve your productivity and profitability into the future.
- Standards may well have improved your business in the past too, had you used them.
- Complacency is a killer of businesses; but strategizing can become an end in itself. Using standards lets you leverage the work of many other organizations, sharing the load and further reducing risk.
- Crowing about the success you have had without standards will not be much help when you run out of cliff.

Oil For The Business Engine

Lacking in glamour but vital to the smooth running of the machine, rarely noticed but touching each component: standards remind me of engine oil, the unexciting product that safeguards the engine in your car. That's how we should think about standards: as an intrinsic part of the business, without which the business may fail catastrophically.

Unlike an automobile engine, businesses don't make easily recognizable noises when they are faulty. We have to learn to recognize the signals of failure, whether these arise in specific components of the business or result from interactions amongst its parts. I've listened to a lot of business engines, and I have a sense for situations where the absence of standards is degrading different aspects of performance. It's not hard to tune into these effects; and once you hear them, you'll want to take action.

Business degradation through absence of standards affects four principal dimensions of the business performance model. These are:
• Operational effectiveness
• Time to market
• Share of channel
• Cost of competence

Operational Effectiveness

Organizations that don't use standards elect to invest in a vast range of wasteful, repetitive activities. These ramify the sludge in their business processes, making their customer service slower, their use of capital poorer, and their people more miserable. The clicking you hear from this business engine is the sound of rekeying as data gets repeated across different systems.

Time To Market

Developing a new product shouldn't mean you have to invent all the components of the product. Imagine if you worked in the electronics industry, and every time you wanted to design a new product you also had to design the resistors and the capacitors, rather than knowing you could source standard components from anywhere in the world. It's the same if you don't use standards in your business. You have to keep re-inventing the wheel, even though wheels aren't your business. Meanwhile, your competitors are out of the gate before you've finished warming up. With the windows of opportunity in the market growing ever slimmer, time to market is becoming a survival issue.

Share Of Channel

Use standards and you widen your field of potential business partners. Avoid standards and you absent your organization from the broadest, and richest, segments of the market. By setting out your stake as a maverick, you are signaling either that you are strong enough and tough enough to own and operate your route to market without partners; or you are stating that the higher costs of doing business with you are justified. Is either of these propositions ever true? You would be right to be wary of the arrogance of any player who believes he can thrive in today's market as a sole provider. Even direct insurers look to outsource some business functions and "white label" others, meaning they're just as connected as everybody else. And if you are going to present partners with interworking costs higher than those of the standards-using community, you had better be able to quantify the additional benefits your lone stance offers. I sincerely doubt you'll be able to make your marginal cost look like a partner or customer benefit.

Cost of Competence

Organizations that do not deploy standards condemn themselves to expensive proprietary systems, work practices and skills that unnecessarily inflate their costs and reduce their flexibility. Where your systems do not use standards, you deny yourselves access to the pool of industry talent and experience that coheres around standards. You have to design and deliver your own training programs, your own development methodologies, and your own documentation management approaches. You have to support the minority skills that are kept alive by a dwindling number of users in the wider market as more and more of your competitors move to standards.

The cost of building specific competence in each of your non-standard processes invests every action point in the value chain with high risk. The business is denied role flexibility, with staff members unable to cover for each other or share high workloads across team boundaries. The organization's dependency on waning technologies, aging systems and arcane schemata puts it at the mercy of supplier failures or price hikes. What may once have looked like a skillfully designed business operation, created to fit the unique circumstances and opportunities of its host organization, begins to resemble a high-wire act performed without a safety net.

Positive Goals

The four dimensions of business performance I've chosen to highlight have associated buzzwords to define the positive goals a healthy organization would set for each. I've held off from using these until now, because I wanted you to share in my horror of the downside of renouncing standards. But if we switch to the positive goals, you'll see how applying standards to each dimension swiftly gets the organization on track for success. In brief, the associated goals are:

• Operational Effectiveness is *customer delight*.
• Time to Market is *organizational agility*.
• Share of Channel is *market reach*.
• Cost of Competence is *knowledge capital*.

Customer Delight

Use standards as a means of ensuring consistently high levels of operational effectiveness. Standards remove duplication and delay from your processes, making your service to customers faster and more accurate. You'll also improve your relationship with business partners, so helping to strengthen the customer relationship throughout the entire supply chain.

Organizational Agility

Use standards to power-up your new product and service development capabilities. Standards let you start the design and build phases of new commercial offerings nearer the point of ultimate delivery. You get to compress the early stages of problem and solution definition by adopting common elements from the standards. You can then focus on what's unique in your offering, directing your investment to where the market differentiation is going to be expressed. You'll be able to act faster and smarter.

"Standards are the product of reason as applied to chaos."

Market Reach

Standards give you access. Buy into the language that everyone is talking and there are more people to talk to. If you're not using standards, you're standing where the market used to be.

Standards enable you to consolidate and apply your expertise – and the expertise of the industry as a whole – to the opportunities around you. The knowledge you have, and the ability to apply it effectively, are the distinguishing features of your business. Most of the underlying transactional processes in our industry have been commoditized, leaving smarts as the source of differentiation and value-add. Standards let you corral, manage and value the knowledge that is at the core of the enterprise's future.

Rationality And Rationalization

When we looked at some of the false alternatives to standards earlier in this chapter, I used the term "justification" to describe the kind of self-deception organizations sometimes use to evade their need for standards. I use this term because it stresses the role of judgment in the process of self-deception. Justification is a creative act of misinterpretation.

Psychologists sometimes use the term "rationalization" for the same process. Here, the "ratio" part of the word means "reason," or a person's mental faculties. But rationalization has a respectable role in the business world too; when the reason being applied is genuine, objective reason. In fact, seeking to make complex or disordered domains rational, *reasonable*, is the function of standards. The rationality we thereby introduce into an otherwise chaotic world is a major guarantor of our ability to act purposefully. When we rationalize our environment, we make it easier to comprehend, navigate and exploit.

For example, we have rationalized systems of weights and measures through international processes, so scientists, manufacturers, suppliers and consumers can all make use of common, objectively defined quantities. By bringing reason to haphazard systems of measurement, ideally through a managed standards process that serves the interests of all stakeholders, we can stabilize vast areas of human interest. Rationalization can also be used to refine the way things are done, as well as the quantities with which we deal. Take, for example, labor in a manufacturing enterprise. A work study allows us to identify areas of specialization within the organization's processes, making its chain of production more efficient, and the quality of its output more consistent. From the crudest division of labor to the most sophisticated job design, rationalization of process adds reason to activity.

Rationalization of quantities and processes both produce standards. Standards are the product of reason as applied to chaos, whether of static classifications (like weights and measures, or currencies) or dynamic patterns (like business processes or mechanical behaviors). The key role of reason demands standards be created and maintained by cooperative bodies. Human intelligence, harnessed to work on a domain of common interest, discovers the order hidden in apparent chaos. Our applied rationality finds the implicit design in disordered activities, and fixes it in explicit models to which other minds can refer.

You can call the process of creating standards one of abstraction, or architecture, or codification. I prefer to call it *thinking hard.* When we apply our experience and our genius to a business domain, and exclude any temptation to justify the historic state of the domain, then we begin to rationalize. We discern the forest, and distinguish it from the trees. We draw a map. We name the features around us. We define tests for acceptable instances of information and examples of behavior. We project our reason on to the business. If this all sounds weird, and philosophical, and a tad dry, consider this: business is only the actions of people dealing with each other. People helping each other, trading their skills and knowledge, building greater value together than they could achieve acting alone. People, people, people. And without reason, we are not people, but cutouts.

Artform of Business

It's worth making this point, because standards are nothing less than the supreme art form of business. By art, I don't mean you'd necessarily want to hang a standard on your wall and invite people over to stroke their beards in front of it. But I do mean standards convey their makers' understanding of the world in which they live, and their communication of how that world can be accessed by others. Like art, standards act as a combination passport, travel guide, money guide and native interpreter to a new world. And that's why standards, the consolidated secretions of many committed minds, are business treasure: engaging, life-changing, and beyond price.

14

Advocacy

Take the standards message throughout the enterprise

A s we've seen, standards follow rationality. Standards develop from a process of rationalization – that is, using our reason. Now, most organizations are led and staffed by people of reason. These organizations don't get the market share and industry respect they command without exercising reason. How is it, then, some leaders seem to be immune to the message of standards? It's not that they "just don't get it," in the patronizing phrase of the most out-there Bubble-era boosters. They get it; but they don't want it.

In situations like this, where decision-makers and implementers agree on the theoretical benefits of standards but shy away from their use, I usually find some poisonous experience in their past accounts for their rejection of standards. An apparent lack of interest in standards can sometimes mask an active antagonism to them. In organizations like this, standards are often a taboo subject. And wherever you find a taboo, you can be certain you'll find some bodies buried close by.

This kind of corporate experience is immensely powerful in setting expectations and behaviors for the future. But before we write such companies off, and assume they will never re-enter the standards world, we need to ask whether their aversion is terminal. I refuse to believe any organization, no matter how standards-shy it is, is a lost cause. To accept such an organization's self-estimation of defeat would be to condemn it to future, systemic, catastrophic failure.

Bad Experiences

First, let's consider the nature of bad experiences. All companies endure bad experiences. No one has a 100 percent success rate — and we're rightly suspicious of any person or organization claiming such a perfect record. The key to organizational success is not avoiding mistakes at all costs, but learning from the mistakes we make. Those organizations that don't learn from their bad experiences become dysfunctional. They become unable to address large areas of business concern: those topics bounded by, or overshadowed by, the topics of past failure. They effectively reduce their scope of activity, painting themselves into an ever-smaller corner.

Most examples of this kind of behavior are simple to spot, and to remedy — though sometimes it takes an external eye to notice the dysfunction. That's why concerned business partners, or consultants, or new hires, often see these issues faster than incumbents do. The effect used to be most obvious in the basic use of information technology. New CEOs would arrive at companies that had mothballed their PCs because of bad early experiences with automating their business processes. Perhaps they'd bought into an operating system that later became insupportable, or bought an accounting package that wasn't open to subsequent modification as the needs of the business changed. The new team member would generally bring a *better* experience of technology implementation with him, and inspire a new vision in the organization. His rival experience would paint an alternate reality in which technology delivered the benefits promised for it. His leadership would recover the earlier spirit of the organization, and purge it of the bitter poison of bad experience.

The myth around standards may be a more subtle quantity. The effects of not using standards contribute to sub-optimal performance on a range of business indicators. Absence of standards produces an overall degradation in performance obvious to users or proponents of standards, but not so clear to the uninitiated. It's not like turning up at a delivery company and noticing they've reopened the stables because no one knows how to unscrew the gas caps on the once-shiny delivery trucks.

So, bad experiences cause a kind of local, self-willed blindness. The *real* problems of the business — the problems standards solve — remain. But these problems are like the elephant in the living room: we're too polite to talk about them.

Implementation

Second, we need to make, and to reinforce, the distinction between standards and *implementations* of standards. A good idea doesn't become a bad idea just because someone, somewhere, at some time, failed to cover himself in glory with a project based on the idea. Ideas are abstract. Good ideas remain good ideas even when immature implementations fail, and fail disastrously. The concept of powered flight seemed ludicrous right up until the moment the Wright brothers achieved their momentous 59-second flight on December 17, 1903 in North

"Good ideas remain good ideas even when immature implementations fail."

Carolina. Even then it took some time for air travel to become a commercial viability and a mainstream mode of travel. How often do we look at prototypes and business models and say: "it'll never fly"? Nice idea: but I've seen a lot of messy crashes.

Good ideas generally trail a string of failures along with them. This is a powerful reason why organizations may reject them. Most organizations do not want to bear the full risk of a new technology or business model. Many of those who do grasp new concepts with enthusiasm fail in the face of the enormous technical challenges involved in transforming a good idea into a profitable product or service.

But wait! Standards aren't weird, unknown, ungovernable creatures. They're tame. They're documented. They come with the testimony and public experiences of those who have already adopted them. Standards are the outcome of risk removal. They're the wisdom that results from the repeated successes of other folks. They're the embodiment of the agreements of other organizations with world-views, and businesses, similar to your own.

When standards projects fail, it is never the standards that are at fault, but the way they have been implemented. It may be the wrong standards have been applied to the problem domain. It may be the project team compromised the integrity of the standards to meet pre-existing architectures or work patterns. Sometimes standards projects fail because the team honors standards in the breach: they pay lip-service to the use of standards, but do not truly incorporate them within the project's work. Companies that don't distinguish between the (honorable and correct) principles of an initiative and its implementation quickly lose the plot — and their place in the market.

Were Standards A Factor?

Third, we need to take care in ascribing the reasons for a project failure to the use of standards per se. This may sound like special pleading, but think of it this way: If a marketing campaign does not produce the results expected of it, we don't blame the failure on "marketing." We don't junk the discipline of marketing and the concepts that go along with the discipline. We look for reasons amidst this particular implementation of marketing practice. Did we have the right offer? Did we select the right target population? Did we make our offer understandable? Did we take into account the offers being made simultaneously to this population by our competitors, and perhaps by other parts of our organization?

The reasons why standards-based projects fail fall exactly into line with the traditional reasons *all* kinds of projects fail. Standards don't add specific risk to a project. In fact, standards de-risk projects. Standards are the least likely component or accelerator of a project's failure to meet its goals. They're more likely to have acted as a brake and a delimiter of negative impact. No decision-maker or leader wants to be a follower of fashion. But why be a follower of failure? Life goes on. Learn what you can, and move on. Encourage people to analyze the mistakes made on a failed project, and consolidate the learning in new processes, procedures or principles that can help you win next time out.

> "If a marketing campaign does not produce the results expected of it, we don't blame the failure on 'marketing.'"

Above all, hold on to the good ideas. If your timing was off with your first implementation, it only means you anticipated the development of your market. And wouldn't you rather be an insightful strategist who got his toes wet a little early than someone with their head in the sand — and their rear end in the deluge when it comes?

Ten Propositions For Standards Adopters

1. All businesses are formed from communicating parts. Some of these parts belong inside the organizational boundary, while other parts lie outside the boundary. Businesses act through the relationships created by this situation.

2. Every business relationship is different and special, but there are common factors in them. When these common factors are recognized and supported by business processes, relationships become easier and cheaper to initiate and sustain, and increase their lifetime value.

3. All business interactions rely on standards of some kind. It makes sense to recognize standards underpin relationships, and to choose the standards with the best fit for your business.

4. The optimum position to take on standards is to be an active member of the group that forms and develops the standards you use, so they meet your needs as well as possible.

5. Business systems should serve business. Systems serve business best when they are modeled according to the needs and opportunities of the business, not the constraints or preferences of technology.

6. Standards should be as simple as possible, but no more so. Good standards are self-explaining to the user group for which they are designed.

7. Competition and cooperation are features of all industries. By supporting efficient relationships amongst industry players, standards promote competition and cooperation in equal measure.

8. Business evolves at many different levels and at many different timescales. Standards need to evolve in step with business evolution.

9. Standards can describe businesses as well as support their efficiency. They therefore supply a common language for strategists, planners and team leaders.

10. Implementing standards fixes current problems, removes future problems and generates larger opportunities for the business. Standards should be regarded as an investment in business processes, knowledge capital and market command.

The Inner Evangelist

In the mid 1990s a new tag started appearing on the business cards of certain senior engineers and marketers in technology companies: *evangelist*. Other types of business begat evangelists too, but the big platform companies took the role most seriously. In the midst of what were (and still are) often dismissed as "religious wars" over the relative merits of competing proprietary computing and networking platforms, the tech companies put their hearts on their sleeves and tasked key individuals with promoting their products full time, expert to expert.

The evangelist's role is to be committed to and excited about the company's product. He is a form of human virus, sent out into the world with infectious enthusiasm. He talks the language of his target audience, shares their goals, values and cultural heritage. He is one of them, but privileged to be a little further along the path to salvation than the members of his audience have reached. He is their pathfinder, their explorer: living proof the Promised Land exists, and is attainable by anyone who seeks it.

The evangelizing organizations have got it right. The human vector is the ideal choice for promoting behavioral change amongst humans. We learn from other people, listen to their stories, try to emulate their success. And in my experience, there's an evangelist in everyone. The inner evangelist may be lying dormant, but he is there. I've yet to meet a single business person who does not harbor the desire to improve the way work gets done, or the scope of the business's opportunities, or the value of its transactions. Disappointment may have taught them outward cynicism. But even distrust of new ideas and new methods can be a strong sign the inner evangelist is about to break the surface. You can't suppress the impulse to do good forever. At some point, it's got to burst free.

Standards often act as the trigger that releases people's inner evangelist. This effect is imprinted in the DNA of standards. Let me explain. People change their thinking when they meet ideas that seem to articulate, or add structure to, concepts already forming in their own minds. We meet successful new ideas half way, and literally recognize them as relevant to our inner worlds. We can change our mental models to accommodate new information because we are already in the process of shifting our mental furniture around, aware — perhaps only subconsciously — that changes in the environment are placing new demands on our ability to respond. Our inner evangelist is often demoted to slumming it as the caretaker of our mental models, worrying at the growing misfit between the repertoire of action we have built up and the new situation brewing in the external environment.

Happily, standards are, by their very nature, articulating, structuring and orienting products. They take the form of conceptual models, and are communicated in simple language. Therefore they match very closely the kind of sustenance our inner evangelist, or mental model caretaker, is most likely to welcome. It's as if the mind has its own set of receptors, to which standards snap like puzzle pieces. To keep mixing my metaphors, standards can act as the switch that lights up a mental model, flooding it with new energy, and fitting it for renewed engagement with the business environment.

Feeding the inner evangelist

• A demoted and demotivated inner evangelist can be revitalized by hope. Expose your mind, and the corporate awareness of your organization, to reputable sources of new techniques and models.

• Focus on the benefits of change, not the difficulties of achieving change. Business changes whether you direct it or not, but if you're not focused in a positive direction, the changes in your own environment will tend towards negative ones.

• Recognize your inner evangelist's hunger for meaning and structure. Take time to consolidate your experiences and look for patterns amongst them.

• Let your inner evangelist speak — let him preach. Share your vision for a better world with colleagues, business partners and customers. By doing so, you'll help to liberate their inner evangelists too.

• Hold to standards as the outer expression of your business ideals. Standards are common, external property open to inquiry and challenge from all quarters. They make our own private values and goals into a project we can share as a family or community.

Attitude Quiz

You know how much you like a quiz — especially one that promises to pop you into a nice little category, and patronize you in the process. Well, I've been studying the great leaders in quizzes, such as *Cosmopolitan* magazine, and as a result of my studies I'm able to present you with a quiz specially tailored to tell you where you stand on standards.

It's a light-hearted quiz, and I wouldn't recommend you use it as part of anybody's annual appraisal, except the CIO's. (Just kidding.)

Check the answers that apply best to you, and then whiz to the end to see where you fit. And if you think of any better responses along the way, feel free to mail them to me at gmaciag@acord.org.

Question 1

One of your people mentions it's difficult to get the information she needs to deal knowledgeably with customers — and her co-workers add their agreement. This means:

a: That system we installed isn't working — another IT foul-up

b: These people need training on the system — another HR foul-up

c: Who are these people again, and what job are they trying to do?

Question 2

A trading partner tells you it wants to transact 90 percent of its business electronically by the end of the year, and partners who don't make the grade will be junked. This means:

a: They've gotten into a bed with a big player who can do all its business electronically, and this is their way of kissing us off

b: We'll go along with this, because they're not going to achieve it and they'll have to drop the goal

c: Do they want us to be in the manual 10 percent?

Question 3

A kid from the IT shop tells you the system he is working on is over 70 percent similar to one he worked on last year, and he's reusing lots of code. This means:

a: Those idiots are building a system we don't need — again

b: This genius is saving us money on the new system — we need more guys like him

c: How on earth can he measure the extent of the similarity?

Question 4

Your systems integration partner pitches you a new solution that is "standards-compliant" and "future-proof." This means:

a: The other clichés will be on the next three slides

b: I'll be safe from criticism if I end up recommending this purchase

c: Which standards and which future do they have in mind?

Question 5

The finance department tells you the exchange rate between the dollar and the Elbonian dinar is 1.768, but that Elbonians will only exchange dinars for dollars if you also treat them to dinner in Dallas. This could jeopardize your plan to hire your favored Elbonia-based business process outsourcing company. It also means:

a: You should never expect a straight answer from Finance

b: You should abandon the idea of outsourcing because it's too complex

c: Would they accept the set menu for dinner, or will they be ordering the specials?

If you scored mostly a's, anger and frustration tend to guide your reactions. You've been let down in the past, and you're nobody's fool. You're more than ready to embrace standards, because standards will allow you to judge ideas, projects and systems with objectivity.

If you scored mostly b's, fear and avoidance are dictating your thinking. You have a strong people orientation, which makes you look for human causes when things go wrong, and for human benefits when opportunities are presented. Standards will help you connect with the combined wisdom and pragmatism of your business community, and provide you with a business-specific language for dealing with problems and opportunities.

If you scored mostly c's, you're one of those infuriating people who answers a question with another question. You're unlikely to respond to any situation with a knee-jerk reaction. Your interest is in the wider parameters of the problem domain from which the question arises. You're responding from a position of reason, rather than anger or dismay. You, sir or madam, are a proponent of standards.

15

Dollars & Sense

You'd expect me to be passionate about standards. What may surprise you is my passion isn't born of a miraculous vision. It comes directly from many years experience working on many different projects with many different people. If you can talk of such a thing, it's a practical passion. And it's a passion that can be communicated in very simple terms.

In this part of the book, I want to show why you need to implement ACORD standards, and why you need to do it now. I'm not aiming to scare you, though some of the implications for the slower adopters of standards are pretty frightening. I'm not going to beat you around the head with high-minded arguments. I'm just going to use some simple math, and some straightforward stories from the people who know our standards best – the folks that are using them to generate savings and win new business every day.

As I write this section, I'm reminded of a phrase the French have for something we've all experienced, but which we have no name for in English. It's called *l'esprit d'escalier*. It literally means "the spirit of the stairs." They're not referring to a ghost who doesn't know how to call the elevator. What they're getting at is the frustrating experience when you think of a killer argument *after* you've left the room. The great point you needed to clinch your argument only occurs to you when it's too late to make it.

I've tried to round up all the great staircase-spirits of the standards movement in this part of the book. I present a collection of clear, and I think devastating, arguments for adopting standards. They are ideas I use every day, and that I urge others to use.

Like all the best arguments, there's nothing devious or tricky about them. But they do owe their power to a standards-oriented viewpoint, which isn't the frame of reference we all necessarily inhabit on a day-to-day basis. My main aim here is to encapsulate the main arguments for standards, so that everyone involved in developing services in the insurance business can grab the standards viewpoint when they need it. And, as I hope I'll prove, the time when you need the standards viewpoint is: any time you plan to make money in this business.

Standards are a business issue. For our industry today, standards are *the* business issue. They help us focus on both the top and bottom lines. And, of course, it all comes down to dollars and sense. Here is what Celent Communications, a leading consulting and research organization, reported in October 2002: Carriers surveyed by Celent either expected to achieve or had already achieved integration efficiencies on the order of 20 percent to 30 percent by using ACORD XML standards. If embraced universally throughout the US insurance industry, the use of standards could save the industry hundreds of millions in technology costs annually.

> **"Standards are a business issue."**

It's hard to argue against such significant annual industry-wide savings. But I think it's the per-company savings that really make people sit up and notice. Reduced costs for the industry as a whole come under the heading of "nice to have." We're all good community players, and we all want what's best for the community. But individual per-company cost reductions in the 20 to 30 percent band are compellingly close to home.

Who would willingly pass on that?

Celent went on to ask why any insurer should be a "first mover" in standards adoption, and provided this answer: "The main reason is to *start saving sooner.*"

The emphasis in that quote comes from Celent, not from me, but I'll echo it to the roof. *Start saving sooner.* Every day that goes by is a lost opportunity for substantial savings.

Other industries seem to get this time-based viewpoint more easily than the insurance business. If you run an airline, you'll be acutely aware that every seat on an airplane that flies without someone sitting on it represents lost revenue. Your company pays hard dollars in fuel to loft that seat into the air, and then throws more dollars at the seat to keep it at a comfortable temperature, stocked with food and shown entertainment. It's criminal wastage to let it fly without a paying occupant. (I've simplified airline economics drastically here, but you get the point.)

Leverage

Every commercial organization shares one scarce resource that can be converted into profit: time. The more time you let slip by without extracting the greatest possible efficiencies from your process, the more money you lose. The best time to implement standards is yesterday. Failing that, today will do.

Organizations that implement standards don't just win on crude dollar savings. They also grab market share. This is because companies that embrace standards wire themselves into larger, smarter markets. They enable themselves to co-work with a greater number and variety of complementary organizations in the value chain. And they extend their reach to wider and more diverse markets. Companies that use standards use them to *win,* and to win big.

> **"Companies that use standards use them to *win*."**

I've also noticed adopting standards is always a smart move for the individual decision-makers who take the step. By bringing standards into your organization and spreading knowledge about their usage and contribution to business performance, you shine a new light on the business that quickly reveals opportunities for savings and for new lines of business.

Standards have phenomenal leverage. They let you take the combined experience and expertise of the entire industry and apply them within your organization to its immediate operational benefit. They also act as an entrance to future benefits, via the enlarged marketplace that standards enable. From the point of view of the individual decision-maker seeking to make a difference to the business, this is heavy-duty firepower that has no parallel inside the organization. There simply isn't any other resource available to you that will provide as much bang for the buck, over so long a period.

> **"Standards have phenomenal leverage."**

Infrastructure

One objection that is often raised against the use of standards is their characterization as *infrastructure.* Now, I don't know why infrastructure is meant to be a bad thing when it comes to business processes, when it's seen as fairly vital in the areas of city planning, or building architecture, or financial markets, or pretty much any other complex endeavor you care to name. Wherever this taboo came from, it now needs exploding.

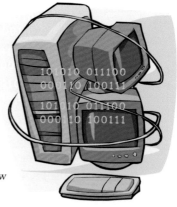

My suspicion is infrastructure projects suffered in the early years of automation, when grandiose platform schemes tended to be long on funding and short on delivery. The heroes of those years were the teams who put point solutions into the business in time to capture business opportunities. The IT profession is around forty years old, and in that short time we've created a neat mythology that labels infrastructure "bad" and solutions "good."

Yet, in the last twenty years or so and increasingly since the dawn of the Internet era, it has become more obvious that the most apparent system disasters are amongst point solutions, while the most obvious winners are found in the infrastructure category of projects. The net itself is infrastructure. So is the web browser, the near-universal user interface of modern times. The Internet's standards – from the tech-level stuff of TCP/IP up to the business lexicons of XML – are all infrastructure. On the other hand, the projects you hear about that break their budgets and fail to deliver on their goals tend to be point solutions, whether they are in Customer Relationship Management (CRM), Enterprise Resource Planning (ERP) or any other Three Letter Acronym (TLA). It's not that every non-infrastructure project is doomed to failure, nor am I claiming that no CRM or ERP project has been a success. It's just that the contributory effect of sound infrastructure is much clearer in today's complex systems environment than it has ever been before.

But you don't really have to buy my arguments on infrastructure. That's because while standards are indeed infrastructure, they're also much more than infrastructure in the accepted sense of the term. Traditionally, infrastructure doesn't extend beyond the organization that commissions and hosts it. A building's heating system does not affect the buildings around it, which remain insulated from it. But business information standards reach beyond the walls of their hosting organizations. Because they are standards, they exist in commonality with all the organizations that use them. This is a form of infrastructure that pervades entire communities, not just single hosts. In other words, rather than being a traditional infrastructure play, implementing standards is actually a *market* play. For the CIO, standards are the key means by which he can effect genuine business enlargement for the company.

> **"Standards are the key means by which the CIO can effect genuine business enlargement for the company."**

Put the time-based viewpoint together with the market-based viewpoint, and you have a double whammy for standards. The first blow gives you immediate, recurring, measurable savings that show up on the bottom line for all to see. The second blow raises your business to a new level of power and potential.

Network Science

There's a fashion today for *network science*, a popularized division of academic complexity theory that looks at the effects of networks. You may have come across the "small worlds" theory that seeks to show how, in a highly connected world, we are all linked in some way with each other. The key phrase here is "six degrees of separation": the idea that we are all connected to each other by, at most, six intermediate relationships. As a standards organization, ACORD is a network enabler. Our standards provide communications pathways that connect our users together and enrich their worlds.

But no network comes into being out of nowhere. Every network is composed of, and animated by, people. The telephone network may be realized in wires and poles and handsets, but it needs people to make it live. It's people who have the language, and the burning need, to communicate with each other. In the same way, whatever the discoveries and the formalizations of network science, it will remain true that networks are enabled by their individual components interacting with each other.

I mention this because although I believe using standards is, in the well-worn phrase, a "no-brainer," I believe that standards can exist or flourish without brains to support them. Standards have an effect on the business world through many individual decisions. Individuals decide buying into a standard will improve their businesses, and by so doing join a community of like-minded decision-makers. And although 20:20 hindsight may show them as being caught in an inevitable wave, the real experience of standards adoption is one of personal commitment and personal action.

"I don't believe that standards can exist or flourish without brains to support them."

Society didn't abandon superstition one morning in some sudden wave of enlightenment. Instead, individuals took separate decisions to reject unreason and adopt the new learning emerging around them. Some individuals took painful decisions in isolation, while others caught the fashion for change around them and changed their worldview with little difficulty. The same kind of process is underway with business information standards – with the difference that waiting around for others to change first can spell doom for the laggards.

16

Managing Change

Breaking the process of change into steps

This chapter is about the reality of change: about making change happen. The core of the message here is concerned with breaking large changes up into small, achievable steps. This shouldn't be a breakthrough notion, but it's surprising how many people reserve the field of business systems from this approach to implementing change. They seem to have the idea systems cannot be broken down and reassembled, or that methods of information transfer and transaction can only be replaced wholesale.

In the first section, we look at the cultural problems associated with managing legacy systems into the future. Then we look at how the incremental approach to change is indeed compatible with major systemic changes. We see how it's possible to retire a well-loved but aging cash-cow business process while remaining in business. We then consider how the incremental approach is used daily in complex businesses where it is seen as the regular, rational way to react to changing requirements. Finally, we pause to muse on business people's attitudes to situations of declining power.

As the world moves on around us, do we try to move with it, or enjoy one last blow-out in the comfort of the era we've grown up in? I believe those who don't embrace standards are celebrating their last party.

Dealing With Legacies

We used to call them "old systems." But that didn't sound polite. So we started calling them legacy systems, and that sounded a lot better. We'd inherited all this old stuff: it was a gift from the past.

"Legacies generally have a value." Legacies generally have a value: they can be liquidated, and turned into some current benefit. If Great Aunt Esmerelda leaves you a hideous armoire, you can always ship it down to an auction house and have it converted into dollars. Take the dollars to Ikea, and you can then complete your intergenerational refurnishing.

The same doesn't appear to be true of soft legacies in the business environment: processes, cultures, and of course software. There's no market in old systems. So how do they comprise a legacy, exactly? Some folks have tried to dub them "heritage systems," which is polite, drops the notion of enduring value, and suggests a museum quality. But I doubt many business people are attracted to the idea of preserving systems just for their historic interest or period charm.

None of these terms really helps us with our systems situation. The reason is "old" and "legacy" and "heritage" all suggest a finality, or a crossing-over between some former age and the current era. The idea running beneath these terms, and which informs our agonizing about legacy systems, is business change brings abrupt discontinuities. The business environment changes, so everything we did yesterday — and therefore are equipped with today — is useless.

People who find this notion attractive like to stress the disruptive nature of new technologies, new competitors, new consumer behaviors. Those who find the idea of abrupt, total change scary prefer to deny the change has happened. They understandably want to cling to what they know best – what works for them. But notice how the welcomers and the deniers alike agree on the binary nature of change. Both groups think either the world is different, or it isn't. There doesn't seem to be a halfway house. It's not Great Aunt Esmerelda, but Hurricane Esmerelda.

The truth is change is a continuous process. Large scale change accretes through a myriad of tiny little changes. There is often a "tipping point" where we recognize the world has taken on more of the character suggested by the large change, and at which time the large scale change appears to accelerate. And certain events can have the effect of symbolizing, and hastening, great changes. September 11 is a key example. The economy was already in downturn before the attacks on New York and Washington, with airlines in particular feeling the pinch. But in retrospect we tend to associate a change in world fortunes with that terrible day: as if the criminal events themselves threw a switch across the economic and political world.

At the level of individual businesses, systems come to be designated "legacy systems" as new technologies reach commercial maturity, or competitors introduce more up-to-date systems. But in fact every system we have ever built, and every system we will ever build, begins to age the moment it is deployed. Just as your new car begins to depreciate as you drive it away from the dealer, so your systems decline. As long as technology continues to advance, this will be so.

> **"Change is a continuous process."**

It's not a popular point to make, but the systems you commission today are the legacy systems of tomorrow.

But let's not despair. There is something you can do to protect your investment in systems. Your systems need not rust away to nothing before they reach the highway. Standards can extend the value and investment of your legacy systems. Here's how.

By basing systems on standards, you base them on a durable and well-serviced foundation. If you use standards, you can shift large portions of your systems to new platforms if better ones become available. You can also modify their functionality to changing business needs without scrapping the entire body of code. Most importantly of all, using business collaboration standards such as ACORD's ensures your systems will be able to communicate with other systems in the business firmament as and when you want or need them to.

Many people I talk with are happy to endorse this point. They agree using standards is the single best way of iron-cladding their systems investment. They even go so far as to agree that business-to-business interoperability, as facilitated by ACORD standards, is synonymous with business continuity. In other words, they recognize abandoning the "legacy trap" is the same thing as avoiding business failure.

Yet these same rational, reasonable folks often have a problem seeing how standards can help them, given they are saddled with a "legacy" ball-and-chain. They can't grasp the future because the past won't let them go. And they assume the same dilemma applies to their peers. The theory is only new entrants, unencumbered by old systems, will be able to start afresh with standards. I hope the logic isn't that our established players should do the honorable thing with a bottle of whiskey and a revolver. There are, I'm happy to say, a great many other options.

To understand how we can take the past with us into the future, we have first to let go of the idea of sudden, discontinuous change. I accept the appearance of a stunning new technology or a super-healthy new competitor can shock us into a sense that times have changed. But such events are wake-up calls, not closing bells. Beneath the excitement generated by symbols of change lie the duller facts of gradual change. And it is this gradual change whose speed and direction we can influence and direct.

The Incremental Mentality

The secret to successful change isn't that much of a secret. You need to do it in steps. It's the old story: How do you eat an elephant? In small bites.[19]

The barriers I see to successful incremental change aren't to do with the technique itself. They are connected with people's feelings about the change process.

In the first place, people often believe "change management" is something done by specialists, and probably by specialists who parachute down from somewhere outside the organization. And change management is indeed often a service provided usefully by external consultants. But any management consultant will tell you it's the organization "doing" the changing that actually has to "do" the changing. External aides can help, but they can't do it for you.

And then there is a series of barriers to change which masquerade as business concerns but which, I'm sorry to say, are really emotional objections. They are closely linked to the binary, all-or-nothing, yesterday-can't-take-us-to-tomorrow thinking that leaves organizations doing nothing in the face of environmental change. Let's look at the two leading manifestations of this unhelpful attitude, which I'll call cow-ism and lemming-ism. (Any resemblance to bulls and bears is entirely intentional.)

Cowism

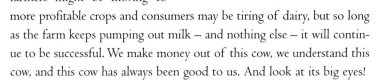

Cow-ism first. Under this doctrine, the organization is happily tending a cash cow and sees no reason to slaughter it. Other farmers might be moving to more profitable crops and consumers may be tiring of dairy, but so long as the farm keeps pumping out milk — and nothing else — it will continue to be successful. We make money out of this cow, we understand this cow, and this cow has always been good to us. And look at its big eyes!

But what's wrong with this picture? It's the fact that some farmer somewhere has switched, and is making money. It seems you can get out of the cow business and survive — even thrive. Furthermore, you know in your heart you can't insist your customers keep swallowing what you push at them. They've got hooves too, and they'll vote with them.

"You can't run a business on stubborn belief."

Organizations that insist their existing products, processes and alliances serve the best interests of their customers in the face of competing evidence have begun to worship their cash cows. You can't run a business on stubborn belief. There comes a time when the cow has to be phased out. In the spirit of incremental change, I'd suggest organizations begin by mixing in a little non-cow business, and changing the mix across several intermediate stages. That way they take their customers with them. And they get to manage the transition at a secure pace, with maximum transparency.

This approach works even where companies seemingly have a monolithic product that won't succumb to incremental change. Say, for example, a company directs all its data exchange through flat files. The arrangement seems to work, it ain't broke so it doesn't need fixing, and the company's business partners aren't complaining. Flat file exchange is an all-or-nothing proposition; you can't mix in a little real-time collaboration. But the incremental steps you take need not be product amendments. They can be product *portfolio* amendments or customer segmentation amendments, or, more usually, both.

By a product portfolio amendment, I simply mean the situation where a company offers an alternate product alongside its existing offering. As well as the traditional flat file service, the company now begins to offer XML connectivity. The company might choose to introduce an incentive for those partners who opt for the XML method, in recognition of the savings it will accrue itself by switching to this channel.

A customer segmentation amendment means we analyze and query our customer or partner base to determine which customers want an alternative to the flat file product. This exercise may produce a ready group of parties avid to make the switch. It is also likely to yield a set of parties who want to make the change, and are looking for guidance from the partners with which they do business. Above all, they may be looking for a timetable for implementation. Our proactive company is now in a position to lead the change and help build the timetable. This way, the trading community works together to retire the cash cow.

Examples of cash cow retirement abound in today's business environment. Cell phone operators want to shift you to digital service, and price and package their digital services accordingly. Cable operators want you to connect to the net via their wires, not the phone company's, and the consumer offers follow. (Admittedly, this is an instance of someone slaughtering a neighbor's cash cow, but you get the point.) State governments who toy with the idea of moving consumers to electric-powered vehicles can use the taxation system to create incentives and disincentives. Stores can give discounts to customers who shop online rather than using a store. And so it goes on: Monolithic user bases with no apparent impetus to change their habits, all moving steadily to an improved situation through co-operative action with a guiding supplier.

Lemmings

Now let's look at lemming-ism. Lemmings are famed for their fol-low-my-leader behavior which sup-posedly sees them committing mass suicide by leaping over cliff edges. People in our industry who are afflicted with lemming-ism say they like the look of standards, but "we're waiting to see which way the industry goes."

Can you see the flaw in this posi-tion? That's right: It's the idea that "the industry" is something outside of its players. But there is no "industry" outside of the people who make up the industry. You mean you want to wait and see what you do yourself? That is weird.

Most lemming-ists see themselves as pragmatic. But when faced with the opportunities and threats of change, the pragmatic response is to design and implement a program of managed, incremental change. If you decide to wait and watch what everyone else does, you are essentially opting to lose out. It's an over-wise approach. People who insist on this position are like investors who won't call the top or bottom of the market, con-

"Most lemming-ists see themselves as pragmatic."

vinced that when it's absolutely safe to do so they will move. But it will only be absolutely clear when the market has changed when... it has changed. If you believe you can hold back your decision indef-initely, then you are making a bet that there will be a crowd of dumber lemmings along after you. You don't need to be first, but you can't afford to be last either.

The all-or-nothing mindsets we've discussed here aren't the only way to do business. They are, as you can see, highly risky, while being cloaked in down home reasonableness. And I think the errors in this thinking can be reduced to two simple falsehoods:

- Cannot take customers with us
- We are at the mercy of vendors

I come across these attitudes all the time and I have to say they are poison to any otherwise healthy business. Take these ideas together, and they add up to an admission of business defeat.

Your customers are immoveable? Oh, no. Your customers are free agents, and one of the directions they can choose to take is *away* from your organization. They don't hang around because *you* hang around. Customers never cite inertia as a reason for loyalty, and if you think they value you for your contempt of their evolving needs and powers of judgment, they're going to give you a nasty surprise. Customers are indeed often loyal beyond the bounds of rational choice, but you should not rely on something so fragile and unpredictable. The reason customers stay with organizations beyond the point of their benefit is usually a lack of knowledge about alternatives. But that knowledge gets out at some point, and when it does it spreads like wildfire.

Furthermore, loyal customers want you to change. They want you to renew the value you represent. They want the choice they made yesterday to be the right choice for today and tomorrow. They don't want to be wrong. They don't want to be inconvenienced by looking for a new supplier. They expect you to absorb the best the industry has to offer, and move with the times.

"Loyal customers *want* you to change."

This is the case with business-to-business customers as well as consumers. You may be trading happily with your business partners using flat file transfers. You may tell yourself you can't afford to change the nature of the working relationship, because your partners will complain about the disruption. But don't you think if you have discovered a change that will benefit both you and your partner today and in the long run, you owe it to him to introduce the change? If you can remodel the costs of the channel for recurrent savings *and* broadened business opportunities for both of you, what right do you have to keep the change from him? It can only be because you're thinking of the transition as an all-or-nothing, zero-sum game. But change is not that kind of big bet. You won't be taking an ax to your business relationships. You'll just be upgrading them, in a steady, predictable, assured style.

At The Mercy of Vendors

But we are at the mercy of the vendors, right? If the people making the systems don't want to bring up standards in polite conversation, then clearly we can't have them, right?

Clearly, if you have a taboo around a subject, then you're not going to make any progress. We project a lot of motives on to vendors, and we're generally wrong. When we looked at countering the contrarian, we noticed how vendors are often accused of "pushing" standards in some obscure hope of monopolizing the systems market — when all open standards do is open markets. And it's easy to hold the opposing view: that vendors don't want to implement standards because they don't want to junk their existing investment in systems. In other words, they want to go on milking their cash cow, and it's impolite to say so.

Nothing could be further from the truth. The software business has bought economist Joseph Schumpeter's concept of "Creative Destruction" by which he describes capitalism and taken it to heart. Vendors know that standards destroy existing products and create opportunities for new products (and services, and indeed businesses). They urgently want to embrace this change. They desperately seek implementation partners who want to embrace the changed world, because without such partners they have no effective presence in the new marketplace. Vendors are not, as a rule, standing on the beach with the legendary King Canute, trying to stop the incoming tide with an imperious gesture. They're waxing their surfboards, hoping for customers.

"Standards create opportunities for new products."

17

The Human Factor

Working together to bring the benefits of standards home

Businesses are made up of all kinds of people. People with different backgrounds, different skills, and different outlooks. Part of the trick of being successful in business is getting your people lined up and pulling the same way – while valuing their diversity.

In this chapter I look at how standards have a meaning for all kinds of groups within our enterprises. Standards aren't just an issue for IT folks and business strategists. Standards are at the heart of each and every mission in today's successful organization. And it's the various diverse disciplines within our organizations that often grasp the case for standards with the greatest clarity, and communicate the case loudly and widely amongst their colleagues.

The underlying theme of this chapter is influence. Influence is the human fuel of collaboration. As individuals, we can achieve great things. But as teams, we can really change the world. It's only by getting other people to share in our visions that we can team up to achieve truly worthwhile goals. If you're inspired by standards, you can translate inspiration into influence, and influence will beget action.

Influence At Large

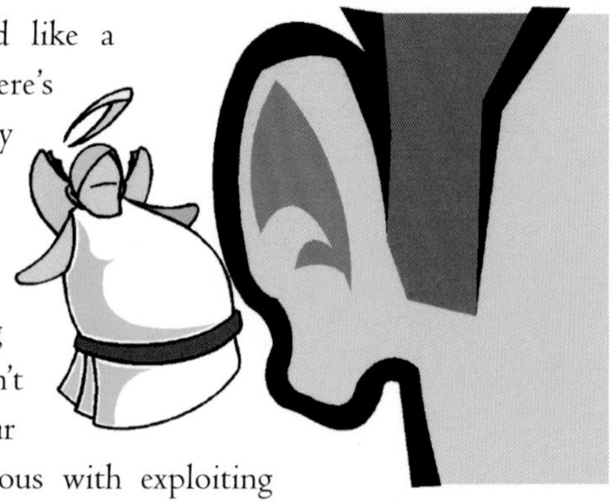

"Influence" can sound like a mystical process. There's something not entirely wholesome about the word. "Influencing" someone can imply conning him into doing something he doesn't want to do. "Using your influence" is synonymous with exploiting your social connections to promote some person or project.

My concept of influence has both integrity and neutral practicality. It derives partly from the well-known Serenity Prayer, attributed to Reinhold Niebuhr (1932):

> God grant me the serenity
> to accept the things I cannot change;
> courage to change the things I can;
> and wisdom to know the difference.

Influence is about creating change. We must all find the courage to influence those things that demand our influence. Stephen R. Covey's "Be Proactive", the first of his famous *Seven Habits of Highly Effective People*[20], develops this idea graphically. Covey describes the "Circle of Concern" that holds our personal interests, desires, worries and fears. He locates a "Circle of Influence" within the larger Circle of Concern. The Circle of Influence contains the issues we can expect to resolve or amend. These issues can be personal ones or ones that connect with other people. Being proactive is the habit of enlarging the Circle of Influence so that it occupies the optimum part of the Circle of Concern.

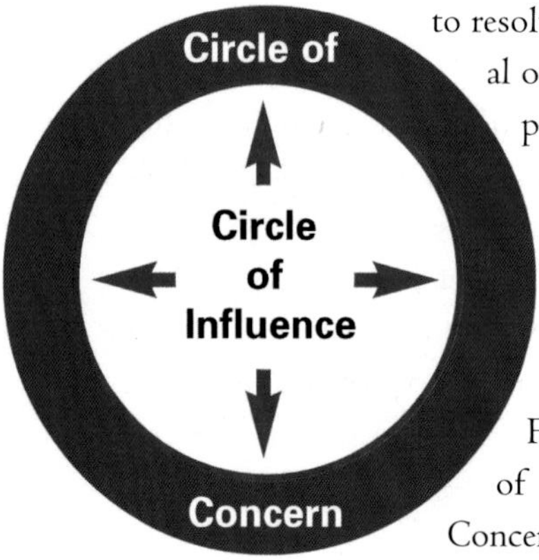

Figure 13: Proactivity enlarges the Circle of Influence to cover more of the Circle of Concern[21]

Recognizing, acting upon and enlarging your Circle of Influence is a legitimate and healthy way of realizing goals. It is, in fact, a kind of moral obligation. Cut the power to your Circle of Influence, and you withdraw from the human project.

In the work context, the efficient and effective interworking of different teams or businesses can often look like something outside our control. Unless you are a geek or a pointy-head you're not going to be able to help. All that stuff is done by computers, and you need to speak Computer to make a difference in that space.

Not so. Business standards such as ACORD's exist to release the business essence from the area of technical endeavor. Standards detach what systems are *for* from what they are built out of. Standards give systems back to the people whom they serve, while leaving the nuts and the bolts and the grease in the workshop.

> "Business standards exist to release the business essence from the area of technical endeavor."

Non-technology people can therefore use standards to enlarge their personal Circle of Influence. You can use standards to exert greater control over the issues that affect you and yours.

I find viewing the world around us in this way helps neutralize one of the ever-present dangers in corporate life. Organizational politics is an inevitable by-product of organizational life. Organizations gather individuals and groups and set them goals. Individuals and groups generate their own goals. Agendas multiply and compete for attention. This is the way human beings are, and it is a vital part of the spirit that makes us achieve great things. But office politics can also poison organizations.

By regarding influence as a means of creating mastery over our concerns, we become clear about our goals. And if we use neutral, collaborative entities such as standards to embody our proactive efforts toward achieving those goals, we avoid the ambiguity and subterfuge that usually accompany political maneuvering. Standards are truly a gift to those who are proactively seeking to improve the world around them without either having to learn everybody else's skills or descend into tactical skirmishing.

Insiders Thinking Outside The Box

Many communities who would benefit from co-operating via standards only wake up to the peril of their shared situation when it is becoming acutely dangerous. Take the ancient Italian city of Venice, where canals act as roads and form the only supply channel. Venice's population has halved in the last twenty years, but boat traffic has doubled as tourism continues to flourish. Meanwhile wash from motorboats contributes to the erosion of the city's ancient buildings.

Fabio Carrera of Worcester Polytechnic Institute in Massachusetts has developed a plan that will cut delivery traffic by 90 percent. By studying the trips taken by delivery boats throughout the city, Carrera has designed a scheme that will, in one drop-off point, reduce the number of delivery boats from 96 to three. The scheme works by routing deliveries according to destination, rather than product. So, instead of the olive oil boat visiting every point of the city, olive oil is carried along with many other supplies on co-operative delivery boats. The plan uses the same number of boats, but has them making fewer trips each. This protects the boatmen's jobs, while the introduction of a centralized warehouse creates new roles.

This is a great example of a designed hub-and-spoke system replacing a messy, point-to-point system that has evolved over generations. The "standards" element can be found in the way the new routes and their loads are defined and implemented. But the aspect of the proposed scheme that strikes perhaps the loudest note is this: "Carrera, who was born in Venice, says dealing with its intricate union politics would have been almost impossible for an outsider."[22]

In other words, no matter how objectively effective a rationalizing scheme is, if the scheme is not created and promoted by the community itself, it will not fly (or, in this case, sail). This is one of ACORD's key strengths. ACORD is not a supplier to the insurance industry. ACORD *is* the insurance industry. At the same time, from the point of view of any one member organization, we have the objectivity, neutrality and authority of a separate body. We're listened to because we know what we're talking about and because we get no percentage in any specific standards project.

Specialists For Standards

Technologists and business strategists seem to be the natural owners of the standards movement. Yet the benefits of standards run across the concerns and activities of any organization. In this section we look at three example groups of specialists: product developers, legal and marketing.

This collection of specialists is by no means exhaustive. As ACORD's work continues I continue to develop insights into the needs and benefits of other groups within the businesses with which we deal. I'm always interested to hear how professionals relate to standards and welcome your input on the integral value of standards in today's — and tomorrow's — great businesses.

Product Developers

Product developers inhabit a mirror world to the one systems developers live in. One of these worlds is marked by the smart use of component models and composition rules to speed up development and generate quick, accurate results. The funny thing is, it's the world of the *product* developers, not the systems folks, that boasts this slick efficiency.

Think about it. Product developers may start with an open mind when they tackle a new project, but they also work to very tightly defined requirements. They know their target market down to the last nub of demographic detail. They know what they're competing against in the market, and they're clear on their goals for substituting, enhancing or complementing their existing product portfolio. And, crucially, they work in terms of features and parameters.

New financial products are composed from pre-existing, proven elements. Product developers combine and tweak trusted elements to create new offers that meet new market opportunities. They work with a kind of mental Lego set. Many of the elements with which they work have behaviors determined by regulators and others by explicit company policy. In other words, product developers act in a largely standardized world. That's what products are: standardized offers.

But look what happens in an organization where the product development team is assembling and adjusting insurance products according to the commercial physics of standards, but the IT team is obeying the logic of ad-hoc development. The "business" team will present its componentized business solution, only to learn that it has no analog in the IT shop. The computer guys are going to craft the systems delivery solution for the new product from scratch. And they call themselves professionals!

It's not always that bad, because many IT development teams have embraced reusable component technology at the desktop and, often, at the database backend. IT teams that are building systems from components will see eye-to-eye with product developers.

Yet there's a level of componentization that isn't always obvious to IT folks, and that's because it's a level not covered by their "integrated development environments" or adequately promoted by the vendors who provide their power tools. This is the level of business-to-business communication. Although IT people are excited by networks, they're often surprisingly ill-informed about the *semantic* level of networks. They don't necessarily know the way systems communicate with each other across departmental boundaries — and between different companies — can be componentized and reused via standards. They often don't realize modern insurance products depend on communication amongst systems as much, if not more so, than efficient use of databases or rapidly produced GUI (graphical user interface) screens.

We've therefore got a situation where product developers are increasingly birthing products that rely on a connected world, but systems developers keep treating the connectivity dimension as a novelty. Some of them have seen what's going on and discovered the vast benefit standards bring to their work. Others haven't. Their suppliers haven't told them, and the IT media prefers to focus on more newsworthy issues, like the latest toys and the latest fallings-out between the big IT players. A great number of otherwise excellent IT delivery professionals are going to keep tripping over this standards issue until some kindly soul on the business side ties their laces for them. Some facts to consider:

- IT people have largely "got" components for developing and reusing screens and databases

- Lots of IT people don't know they can componentize the business connectivity dimension of their systems through standards

- Product developers can show their IT colleagues the way

The Product Developer's Show And Tell

Let your IT colleagues know how much of your projected future business is designed to cross departmental and organizational boundaries. Calculate and communicate the gross value of all non-independent products; that is, the aggregated value of all those products that rely on business connectivity between departments or business partners. Introduce your developers to the ACORD standards and process. Mandate the use of ACORD standards for all product system solutions created inhouse or acquired from external sources.

Partner-Enable

I know the insurance and technology industries are adept at producing new terminology, but sometimes you just have to bite the bullet and add your own coinage to the language. I'm humbly going to offer this term: partner-enable.

You already know product development and deployment windows continue to shrink. It's already a challenge to create and launch new products into a highly competitive market. You must increasingly demand your systems providers keep up with the fast pace imposed by the market. You need IT to respond with *market-ready* solutions to your needs. The best IT teams are achieving this goal through the use of component technologies.

But the growth of complexity and diversity in insurance provision also means more and more parties are becoming involved in the conception, underwriting, selling and execution of insurance products. There's a greater crowd of people trying to wedge their combined offering in the shrinking window of opportunity. So your systems not only need to be market-ready in short order, they also need to be amenable to cooperation with business partners. They need to be partner-enabled.

> **"ACORD standards provide a way of partner-enabling systems."**

ACORD standards provide a way of partner-enabling systems. The standards can be used retroactively to make existing systems available to business-level interaction, or used in the construction of new systems to bake interoperability into the solution from the start. In most cases it's a little of both, since many of today's solutions involve combining pieces of legacy systems across a number of different partners with fresh components and wrappers.

Why is this so important? Because the majority of IT systems we're commissioning and building today to meet product development requirements are fundamentally rooted in the interconnected nature of the *industry* we're in.

The Wind Tunnel

Rapid prototyping tools and techniques allow IT specialists to produce prototypes of new systems very quickly. They can use GUI development kits and pre-built business components to construct working systems that demonstrate how a solution will look and feel. Such prototypes can also

function as test environments, capturing and processing real data and providing guidance as to the technical requirements of the full-scale solution.

However, such prototypes rarely model the business-to-business connectivity dimension of a system. Where a new system has to communicate with an existing inhouse system, the prototyping team may mimic the interaction or, at a pinch, build a bridge to an offline version of the cooperating system. Where the system has to communicate with parties outside the organization, the team will rarely venture beyond mimicking the expected interactions.

Using ACORD standards allows prototypers to plug this important gap in their working models. They can use standard interfaces to generate lifelike behaviors for external systems. They can even use standards to build genuine prototype gateways to the systems of the company's business partners.

We can no longer leave the proof of business-level connectivity out of the prototyping stage. If your project needs a proof of concept stage, think carefully about which concepts you're trying to prove. Do you need to prove you can build a good user interface or efficient database management layer? Probably not. But do you need to know whether your new system will work with the other vital systems it needs to deliver its overall objective? You bet.

The system prototypes we are used to are rather like model cars in a wind tunnel. They tell us how a product will stand up to the rigors of operation. But we can't drive those products anyplace. We never needed to study that aspect before, because we could drive our products anywhere we wanted: we built the roads.

Today, our products are increasingly designed to negotiate all kinds of links, not just smooth, straight roads laid out by the sponsoring company. Our prototypes therefore need to give us feedback on their ability to survive different types of connection, different types of terrain.

The good news is the use of ACORD standards in prototypes not only tests the business connectivity dimension of a proposed solution. The standards also re-pave the "wind tunnel" with a reliable road surface. By using standards, we're buying into universality. We're helping to ensure our products really can drive anywhere on the planet.

Marketing

I don't blame marketers for glazing over when standards are mentioned. The way data is framed, packaged and sent flying around the business world's systems seems a million miles away from the concerns of professional marketers. Data doesn't touch people, so it can't be relevant, right?

There are three great reasons why marketers should cheer for standards. I don't expect any marketer worth her salt to pore over the details of ACORD's standards or endure a protracted technical discussion on how they are implemented. But every marketing professional in the business will want to add their backing to these benefits of standards:
• Access to wider channels
• Better direct marketing
• Better market image

Access To Channels

Business connectivity standards join companies together and let them share data. That means partners can create joint marketing programs with ease and accuracy. Marketers can put together different providers to offer highly sculpted offers. Without standards, it's still possible to line up a variety of providers and create a distinctive joint offer. It's possible, but it isn't likely. Do it once without standards and you may never do it again.

Standards provide a universal "plug-and-play" capability at the business level. Every partner that uses standards can interact efficiently and effectively with every other standards-enabled partner. Speak the same business language, and you and your partners can do great business together – even if you don't have existing, deep structural relationships. The cost and uncertainty traditionally associated with ad-hoc marketing combinations melts away as standards provide for universal connectivity at the business process level.

> "Standards provide a universal "plug-and-play" capability at the business level."

Your markets literally expand when your organization buys into standards. And since it's the goal of marketers to create markets, that's great news.

Better Marketing

We stress the value of standards in enabling business partners to work together. But they also have a valuable role to play within the organization, helping disparate systems talk to each other — without producing gibberish.

How many direct marketing projects have failed to meet their targets not because the offer was bad, or the data was inadequate, but because the organization could not marshal all the data it needed or reconcile differences between the different systems providing the data? This situation is so common many organizations restrict their database marketing activities to what they *can* do rather than what they *want* to do. And they impose this restriction on themselves almost thoughtlessly. After all, if the computer guys can't give us what we want, what's the point of making a noise about it? Market opportunities for great customer offers won't wait for the systems people to sort themselves out, or even give them the time to learn how to speak plainly to "the business." Best to make do with what we've got.

Using business standards such as ACORD's will raise your IT game to a level where systems talking easily and meaningfully unto systems is the norm.

> **"Standards help the organization reach the holy grail."**

All the organization's customer data will become available to each campaign. Standards help the organization reach the holy grail of every marketer: the complete view of the customer.

Even better, by using industry standards to achieve this interoperability, the organization gets the benefit of greater compatibility with external systems as a free benefit. This may not sound like a big deal until you consider how marketing partnerships and company acquisitions frequently lead to sudden influxes of customer records that are unusable by the marketing department. The enlarged pool of prospects may have been trumpeted as the prime piece of commercial logic behind the deal itself; yet marketers cannot deliver on that logic because of incompatibilities at the technology level.

The more companies sign up to use standards, the easier it becomes for them to realize customer-base goals when they combine. I accept a belief in company acquisitions may not seem an exciting driver for standards adoption. But I believe the main driver of marketing success has to be the acquisition of prospects. Enlargements of the prospect pool are increasingly made in quantum leaps as companies merge or agree to work together. It is therefore in the interests of us all to use standards.

Better Market Image

This marketing benefit of standards often overlaps with the interests of investor relations specialists. Whether you are a general marketer or part of an investor relations team, you will want to present a well-informed, well-connected image to your stakeholders. By using business connectivity standards you communicate your organization's committed role in the evolving business landscape. You signal you are here to stay, and that you're moving with the times.

As a member of the standards community, you locate yourself within the smart mainstream of your industry. The strategic credibility of other members casts a reflective glow on your own organization. You align yourself with the cost busters, the product innovators, and the agenda setters.

Involvement in the standards movement communicates two valuable facts about your organization that are otherwise difficult to convey. Furthermore, these vital twin attributes can easily be seen as contradictory, and therefore cancel each other out. In the context of standards, this virtuous pair remains in a harmonious equilibrium. They are the attributes of being mainstream and being at the leading edge.

Contradictory? Ordinarily, it's hard to claim your organization is simultaneously in the mainstream and in the lead. But using business connectivity standards really does confer both positions on the organization. The nature of standards is they are widely endorsed. *Connectivity* standards are also future-oriented, expansive, and adaptable. I know of no other business artifact that can bring these otherwise self-neutralizing benefits to an organization.

Professionals addressing investors and opinion-formers will be particularly interested to underline standards' contribution to the organization's investment in infrastructure. Organizations are increasingly rated on their ability to respond rapidly to new business climates, and investing in infrastructure is one way they can publicly demonstrate their embrace of this challenge.

Peter Schwartz, lead author of the influential book *The Long Boom*[23], puts it like this in his latest guide to our economic future:

> Improvements in infrastructure "work" to build wealth because they promote productivity. [...] They also promote globalization. [...] But infrastructure improvements have other benefits as well. They create a platform for stable, reliable connections among people. Those, in turn, make trade easier. They give people the wherewithal to beat back the harsh vagaries of fate. (A viable insurance industry is a form of infrastructure; without it few businesses could survive the risks of investment in potentially dangerous new technologies or new foreign markets.)[24]

Market Opportunities

Why do non-IT people need to influence the use of standards within the organization? Surely that's someone else's job.

The fact is, we all need to support and nurture standards, whoever we are and whatever our formal role. That's because standards affect us all. Furthermore, some of the major business benefits of standards can be invisible to IT experts. This is not because they are insensitive to business issues, but because there is often an unspoken misunderstanding about what is *normal and obvious* between IT teams and business teams.

One way to understand this mismatch in thinking is to approach it from the angle of business triggers. Let's use the example of a market opportunity trigger. In simple terms, a market opportunity triggers two requirements in an organization's systems response: speed, and accuracy. (We'll leave aside the specific requirements of the opportunity in terms of function and data).

Market Opportunity

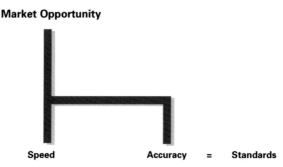

| Speed | Accuracy | = | Standards |

Figure 14: Simplified Market Opportunity Trigger

The requirements for speed (of delivery) and accuracy on the part of the system that will meet this opportunity add up to a call on standards. Since standards already exist, and encapsulate many person-years of labor in the business domain of interest, they give any project a head start. And since standards provide a blueprint for building a major dimension of the system, they also ensure a high degree of accuracy through the removal of semantic ambiguity and the delivery of a common terminology to the project.

The mismatch occurs in this situation because IT teams often only hear "speed" as a requirement to market opportunity triggers. Business customers frequently do not mention accuracy as a requirement because, in the business world, it's normal and obvious that you get things right rather than wrong. There are no pure business projects based on the principle that the core subject matter will be vague. And I have yet to encounter a business project where specialists were encouraged to willfully misinterpret each other's terms.

"Non-IT projects conform to regular standards as a matter of course." Yet the semantic transparency and correctness of systems is *not* always a given in IT teams. It is possible to create a perfectly adequate IT system whose semantics is impenetrable to any outsider — whether human or machine. No non-IT project would or indeed could use the same logic. Non-IT projects rely on open standards such as spoken language. They may also use standards such as laws or regulations. Non-IT projects conform to regular standards as a matter of course. IT projects, on the other hand, have a history of being inspected and manipulated by their builders alone. The world of standalone systems is, however, gone. I cannot think of a single business systems function we could specify today that we could guarantee will never have any interaction with another system.

Business representatives rarely give a thought to specifying semantic accuracy in systems. From their point of view, there is no kind of solution that does not stand up to external scrutiny or challenge, and which is hence, by functional definition, articulated through some kind of shared standard. The business representative's work does not include the option of ambiguity, loose definition, selective or inaccurate structuring.

Confronting this issue head on is likely to lead to unhelpful conflict. But since the solution to the mismatch is encased in standards, promoting the use of standards in a project can neutralize the mismatch before it does any material damage.

It is worth extending our model of market opportunity triggers, because there are increasingly three systemic implications of such triggers rather than two:

Market Opportunity

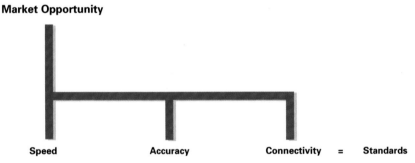

Speed   Accuracy   Connectivity   =   Standards

Figure 15: Extended Market Opportunity Trigger

As we have implied, we now expect connectivity as a basic property of our business systems alongside speed of delivery and accuracy. The period of 1996 to 2000 made an issue of connectivity, sacrificing speed of delivery while Web functionality, development platforms and IT skills caught up with the potential of the Internet. The attention paid to the requirement for connectivity tended to suppress attention to the semantic requirement of accuracy. However, the development of XML solutions has been a means of encapsulating and enacting the benefits of semantic standards, which in turn supports the requirement for business-level connectivity. So, standards that are today encased in XML

meet the needs for speed, accuracy and connectivity in a well-support-
ed, easily adopted format.

"The triple nature of standards – speed plus accuracy plus connectivity."

Those who specify business requirements within a systems project can dramatically improve those projects by insisting on the semantic benefits of standards. We can afford to lessen our emphasis on the technical achievement of connectivity, since this requirement has been met architecturally by a number of technologies, not least in recent years by the proliferation of web services technology. We can also afford to reduce our emphasis on the importance of time to market, since even the most isolated of IT teams has got the message that delivering late to an upcoming market opportunity is equivalent to complete failure. But the triple nature of standards such as ACORD's – speed plus accuracy plus connectivity – ensures if you target one of these dimensions within a call for standards, you will achieve the other two as well. The semantic correctness and integrity of your systems create their business value, and make that value amenable to co-operative uses in other systems and with trading partners. Focus on this requirement as your chief demand of the IT response to market opportunities.

■

18

Change Agents

Strategies for introducing change

This chapter has three parts. The first part is about the differences of viewpoint between people in "IT" and people in "the business." In one way it's a continuation of themes we have explored elsewhere. I believe it is vital for those of us interested in using standards and promoting their dispersal to understand the typical viewpoints of the gatekeepers we meet along our journeys. When we understand each other's points of view we can activate our influence more accurately.

The second part of the chapter looks at specific opportunities that arise within the life of an organization that can be used to introduce standards. The accent is on using events and related business themes to reveal a consensus for the standards-based approach. In this way standards emerge naturally as a healthy part of the organization's development, rather than being seen as an alien bolt-on being urged by outsiders.

The final part of the chapter addresses the role of data standards in protecting data from erosion, corruption or misuse.

Understanding Each Other

Having worked in the gap between IT and "the business" for my entire career, I've gained some insights into the ways the two groups tend to see themselves, and how they tend to regard each other. I'm generalizing when I share these insights, but I believe most people involved in either side of the business-IT equation will recognize the characteristics I'm about to describe.

Let's take the IT team first. IT faces off to a vague entity called "the business," whose traditions and goals the IT folks only loosely understand. The IT team's drivers are much easier to determine and label:

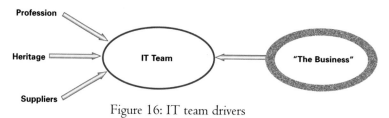

Figure 16: IT team drivers

Switching to the business side, it is safe to say most business people are vague about what drives IT people. The spread of PCs and connectivity into every area of life does not seem to have helped matters, since IT folks often seem to discount business people's experience from other areas. But business people have clear drivers:

Figure 17: Business team drivers

The fact that business and IT teams do not share the same drivers is not a problem. These are different groups that we would expect to be motivated in different ways. However, the ability for people on either side to appreciate the drivers of those they face off to can help cement the work-

ing relationship. An appreciation of this kind can remove suspicion and free resources for focusing on the vague entities that really concern us all as employees: our customers and our trading partners. These significant parties are often buried within a larger cloud known simply as "users":

The first step toward business and IT people appreciating each other's strengths is a recognition that professional loyalties operate on both sides. A business team member's identification with, say, the marketing profession is as real, compelling and influential as an IT team member's identification with, say, the software engineering discipline. Mutual respect in this area immediately removes some of the typical communications problems across the business/IT gap.

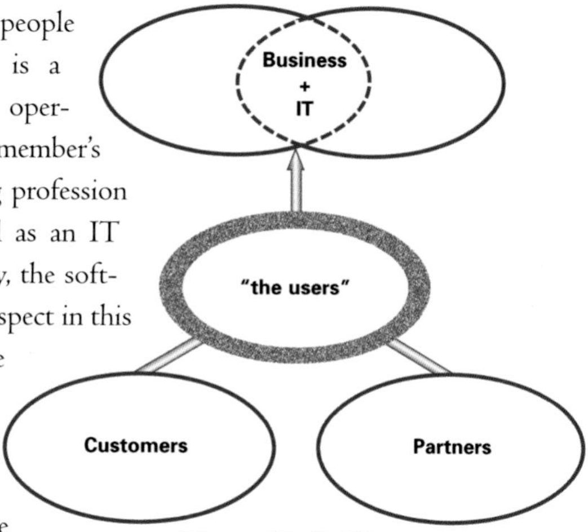

Figure 18: Shifting attention to the real issues

The next step is to match minds on the external influencers who loom largest for each group. For the IT folks, this is the suppliers. For the business folks, it's the competition. Each of these external groups generates an agenda that challenges the autonomy of the internal group. Business decision makers are diverted from their own plans when they have to respond to competitive actions. Furthermore, they must build flexibility to deal with competitor actions into all their plans. This is one of the very good reasons why business plans are rarely "set in stone." On the IT side of the house, suppliers understandably push their own product and service strategies, and may even promote their own industry alliances. IT team members have to sort the useful from the purely promotional in every message they receive from the supplier community. They also rely upon their suppliers for continued support of the goods and services in which they invest on behalf of the organization. IT's relationship with the supplier community is therefore every bit as sophisticated as the business's relationship with its competitors. If colleagues across the business/IT divide can recognize they face equally demanding, if different, external pressures then they can begin to understand areas of reticence or reluctance to commit on either side.

> "Installed systems create an unavoidable bias toward conservatism."

The final thread where business and IT can usefully align is perhaps the hardest to negotiate. This thread is the attitudes to change held by each team.

I believe the burden of installed systems creates an unavoidable bias toward conservatism in IT teams. This may sound odd, since many IT folks are avowedly radical. And IT people are often accused of wanting to build systems from scratch without respecting existing assets. Yet the practical outcome of the majority of IT projects within even the smallest organization is a small revision to an existing system portfolio. It is rarely possible, technically, economically or politically, to scrap existing systems capabilities and start afresh. It's also worth remembering that conservatism is a virtue in the systems world. We want reliability and security from our business systems, and strategies that refuse to play fast and loose with the installed technology base are the best guarantor of such a situation.

"On the business side, I believe we usually find a bias towards radicalism."

On the business side, I believe we usually find a bias towards radicalism. This is because business folks are driven and judged according to business goals; and business goals are all future-oriented. We ask our people to deliver sales and savings. We bid them enter new markets and take targeted share in them. We ask them to go forward.

The enduring reality of IT's position as a support function is no clearer than in this distinction. In order to embrace radical change, IT must respond with cautious change. This is a genuine impedance mismatch.

"Standards represent a pre-emptive strike at the unknown demands of tomorrow."

But there is a way around this mismatch and it lies, not surprisingly, in standards. IT departments that use standards build a high degree of flexibility to change into their systems. Standards represent a pre-emptive strike at the unknown demands of tomorrow. And since standards entail a way of creating systems rather than being a cosmetic add-on to systems, they are also deeply conservative. For IT professionals, using standards is akin to buying insurance.

Standards make organizations future-ready. They also preserve the utility of existing software assets by providing a business-oriented architecture through which those assets can be functionally identified, assessed and valued. In other words, standards have a major role to play in recognizing and managing the dilemma every successful IT department finds itself in: owning twin roles as custodian of the past and pathfinder to the future.

Opportunities For Influence

The most effective form of influence may be a steady, constant pressure. For example, we know the best way to change the behavior of people around us is to model the behavior we want them to exhibit. It's called leading by example.

But for many specialists within organizations, exerting influence on key issues of corporate survival growth such as the adoption of standards is not necessarily a continuous process. One effect of having different disciplines working together in our organizations is they work for much of their time in isolation from each other, coming together at significant touchpoints but otherwise respecting each other's professional space. Someone in, say, marketing may have no day-to-day relationship with colleagues in the systems department.

Many mature organizations have recognized the dangers inherent in this separation of functions. They have learned to their cost that if the bridges are not kept open between their specialist functions, the times when they need to work together erupt into conflict — fueled by misunderstandings and suspicions whose basic origin is in a simple lack of familiarity at the personal level. These organizations create internal "account managers" or "interface managers" specifically to nurture, repair and enrich relationships across functional boundaries.

Folks in this position are ideally suited to maintain a constant, though friendly, pressure on the need for standards adoption throughout the organization. These remarkable people can create a climate of progressive opinion, almost as a by-product of their "official" duties. When you are responsible for managing interfaces, it is hard not to recognize and promote the organizational, process and bottom-line benefits that standards bring.

Where such interface management roles do not exist, specialists who recognize the value of standards have to take whatever opportunities they can to influence others in the decision-making chain. These opportunities are more extensive than you might think. I explore a few of them here, though I'm sure you can think of many more.

Project Initiations

Involved in the launch of an IT project? Traditionally, "users" have been co-opted on to the boards of systems projects to stand proxy for their colleagues in verifying requirements. Increasingly the user representative's role has mutated into principal tester. I believe this is often a misuse of this team member's expertise. For a start, we should see this member as a business representative, not a "user." And we should listen to their business perspective as it applies to the *context* of the project, not just the *content* of the system.

Think about it: We expect our co-opted businessperson to vouch for the accuracy of the system's stated requirements. Should we not also respect and act upon the business context those requirements serve? Especially if the context suggests the requirements should be addressed in a particular way.

> **"The benefits of standards are, above all, business benefits."**

The benefits of standards are, above all, business benefits. Standards save money. Standards drive revenue. Standards underwrite market expansion. Standards reduce risk. You'll notice there's not an ounce of binary or the shadow of a pixel in any of those statements.

A business representative attached to a systems project has the ideal opportunity to assert the best business interests of the organization against the technical constraints that define the world of her IT colleagues. Business standards such as ACORD's embody a set of generic business requirements every bit as fundamental as the technical parameters that define the IT team's capabilities.

The first and best place to introduce this argument is at project initiation. I don't suggest business representatives walk into the first project meeting, demand standards are used, and then clam up. (Though if you try this approach, do send me the photographs.) However, it's reasonable for a business representative to point out that if the combined team had a common vocabulary to use when discussing the goals and requirements of the project, then communications would be much easier. Standards often perform this low-pressure role in projects, providing a dictionary but not threatening the expertise or preferences of the IT specialists. Such uses of standards allow teams to experience the content and usefulness of standards. This experience changes their attitudes to standards, and makes them much more receptive to implementing the standards throughout the project – from statement of requirements to delivery of working system. And then the idea will have come from the IT department, not the business. But you can live with that.

ACORD Best Practices for Standards Implementation

1. Information & Technology Strategy

Incorporate ACORD data standards into your business and IT strategy. The use of the data standards should be a requirement throughout the business, because the data and information flow is the business.

2. Oversight Committee

Create an oversight "executive committee" that actively promotes and monitors the participation, integration and implementation of ACORD standards within the organization.

3. IT Principles

Use ACORD standards as part of your organization's IT operating principles and project management principles. If a project does not include the use of the ACORD standards, it should be seriously questioned.

4. Solution Providers

Demand the use of ACORD standards with your vendors/solution providers and build it within the contracts. You are the customer and you should demand what you need for your strategic future.

5. RFP's

Include the requirement for ACORD standards in your Request for Proposal or Request for Information documents.

6. SLA's

Incorporate ACORD standards as a part of your Service Level Agreements (SLAs) with outsourcers or shared service providers. The lack of ACORD standards will limit your business options and flexibility while placing the power in the hands of the vendor.

7. Foundation for Architecture

Use ACORD data and messaging standards as a foundation for your enterprise data and messaging architecture as well as your data warehouse strategy.

8. Internal and External Integration

Use ACORD data and messaging standards for both internal and external integration between: internal corporate entities, internal systems, trading partners, and third-party providers.

Corporate Rethinks

Modern organizations reinvent core aspects of their operations and methods on a regular basis. Some of these changes are purely functional, such as realignments of operating units to create efficiencies. Other changes are "hearts and minds" initiatives aimed at improving the organization's soft skills or enhancing its image. This latter kind of change offers ideal opportunities to introduce business standards to an organization and lobby for their implementation.

Most "hearts and minds" initiatives focus on areas that are part and parcel of standards' business benefits. Take, for example, those change projects aimed at improving quality. Theory and practice in quality management are subject to continual refinement, as are the ways in which quality's benefits are presented to team members. But certain themes such as awareness of accuracy and commitment to improvement remain constant across the quality movement. Standards share these characteristics, and can be legitimately regarded as tools of the quality movement.

We do not label standards as a "quality issue," because to do so might isolate standards as an aspect of the quality movement, and detract from the value of standards in business survival and growth. I know quality experts chaff at the ghettoization of their movement too, since quality is clearly a concept that runs through every successful organization and is hardly an optional extra in today's highly competitive and demanding markets. But there's no doubt "quality" often acts as a rallying cry to concerted change in a way "standards" somehow doesn't. (Maybe it's the word. Maybe we should change it to "chocolate.")

Brand

Another "soft" area for corporate change initiatives is brand. At first glance it may appear business standards have little to do with brand. After all, surely brand is all about exterior communication — the organization's façade — while standards are about internal stuff: how the engines work, and so on. In fact, any brand expert worth her salt will tell you successful brands represent real values and real activities. They are not spray-on coatings that can be used to hide poverty of ideas, inadequate service or poor quality products. Where a branding exercise seeks to highlight an organization's commitment to customer knowledge or operational efficiency, the message that standards are being used to deliver those goals helps to show more than words are at work in the initiative. If your organization is adjusting its brand to suggest, for example, a greater attention to personal understanding of customer needs, then data standards will demonstrate a practical implementation of this commitment. By adopting the industry's standards for dealing with the information that is dear to the industry, you are making so much more than a gesture. You are walking the talk.

Post-Mortems

Healthy organizations learn from their mistakes. And the more successful an organization is, the more mistakes it makes. That's because successful organizations try out new ideas, new people and new channels. All the time. They manage the risks of innovation, knowing without an open attitude to change they condemn their businesses to decay and dissolution.

Following a failed project – in any area of the business, not just IT – the organization can do one of three things. It can look the other way, silently construct a taboo around what just happened, and carry on as if nothing has happened. Alternately, it can indulge in a blame storm, distributing a few slaps and terminations here and there, and (this time noisily) constructing a taboo around what just happened. The third, healthy way of responding to a failure is to hold an objective enquiry, analyze what happened, and suggest some ways similar failures can be avoided in the future. This type of enquiry also frequently produces learning points that can be used widely within the organization as well as specific "save" advice for future eventualities.

Every internal post-mortem in every organization under the sun would immediately benefit from the inclusion of one question in the enquiry's guidelines: Could standards have helped us here?

So many project failures write up "poor communications" as their chief killer that standards must have a prominent role in the saving of an unimaginably high number of failures-in-waiting. The standards in question will vary in their nature. It may be, for example, that a simple agreement of a few key terms between co-operating teams could have prevented catastrophic failure. But wherever a system using insurance data is implicated in the failure, it's a safe bet ACORD standards will be key to prevention of future failures.

It may not be that for every enquiry you can put your hand on your heart and say: If we'd had ACORD standards on this project, the project wouldn't have gone wrong. But I wager the following statement is true across all such projects: If we'd had ACORD standards on this project, we'd have known the project was going wrong.

A subtle difference? Only if you regard the difference between awareness and ignorance of impending doom as a trivial matter.

> **"Standards build a sophisticated but clear set of reference points."**

The use of standards builds a sophisticated but clear set of reference points into every project in the domain they treat. Standards provide fixed points in an otherwise turbulent sea. They let you know what you're arguing about. They show you where you are deviating from your course. They don't get lost, or obscured, or transformed into something else. They are the project's truest, most constant, friends.

Not Easy to Explain

When the organization responds to regulatory demands for standardization, or competitive pressure to adopt a standard, they can be useful opportunities to consolidate the advance of the general standards cause, and of business standards in particular. The standardization underway may appear to be far removed from the concerns of ACORD's standards. There may be little in common at first glance.

But when standardization is in the air, the generic benefits of standards become a part of the organization's intellectual climate. Implementers may question the purpose of the standardization on which they are engaged, and hope to receive compelling reasons from their leaders. Standards may be "sold" inside organizations in a number of ways. "It's the law: we've got to do it" always works well. But so does this: "The standards will let us throw out the forms (or tasks or costs or suppliers) that we created for ourselves and use the same ones everyone else is using." Whether you are contemplating using the dollar rather than the Elbonian Dinar or stocking the copier with US Letter rather than the triangular stock you've always bought from the guy down the road, your organization is essentially seeking the common ground and the simple benefits of conformity. There are places where you need to innovate, but the voltage running to your power outlets isn't one of them.

> "Standards may be "sold" inside organizations in a number of ways."

Each time an organization introduces a standard — in *any* area of the business and under any rationale or pressure — the inherent, general and unassailable benefits of standards are confirmed for all to see. At these times, your audience is receptive.

I accept business data standards aren't always so easy to explain as other standards. They don't relate to objects you can see and touch. But I notice electrical standards or construction standards are similarly "soft," even though they apply to the physical environment. Maybe, as laymen, we respect such standards because although we may not understand the physics and engineering principle involved, we know what it's like to receive an electric shock or have a wall fall down on us. We have an instinct for such things; but not for data.

Key Strategy

Make the use of standards throughout the organization your expectation. Make it clear that you expect relevant standards to be a part of any project in any area of the organization's activities. Show that the organization cares equally about standards for its electrical wiring and its hiring processes, its bookkeeping and its furniture. The use of standards is your de facto standard.

Does Business Blunt Data?

Data is at the core of every business. And data is inviolable. I appreciate data lives in a context. But that doesn't mean the value of data standards can be eroded by the usages to which they are put. The point about stan-

SENDING DATA . . .

dards is they enable data to move across different contexts, and *protect* the integrity of data from the environments in which it finds itself.

The same is true for money. You could argue a fistful of dollars is doing a different job if it's being bet on a horse, paying for a desalination plant or compensating an airline pilot. Money operates in a bewildering variety of contexts. It is part of the life of the planet.

But we don't need different kinds of money for different activities. Money isn't soiled, degraded, altered or fragmented by any number of transactional events. It's precisely money's persistence that makes it useful in a limitless variety of settings. And whenever we find restrictive currencies, we recognize their limitations and the abuse of power that usually goes along with those limitations. Would you be happy with being paid in funny money you could only redeem in the company store?

> **"Standardized data can be read, transformed and acted upon by a theoretically unlimited number of systems."**

Furthermore, if you roll your own data definitions you are putting up a sign that says you will not accept anyone else's data. Unless you share a standard with your trading partners, you are erecting a barrier to working with their data. And since data is at the heart of all business processes, you are taking an ax to your potential revenue streams.

Bridging

Some organizations argue they can build data bridges between systems and to their trading partners as and when the need arises. This strategy has the apparent virtue of delaying investment in a capability until there is a proven need. However, this strategy rarely works in practice. It's like saying you'll wait till you see a really big rain cloud before fixing the roof. In the meantime you're getting all that extra sunshine for free, so why complain! The problem is, it's hard to specify exactly when the downpour will hit, or how strong it will be. It is also extremely unlikely you will be able to patch the roof in the time you have available. Be honest, you aren't going to keep your people in a state of advanced readiness, primed to act at a moment's notice. You'll be using them for something else.

Actually, the situation is worse than my little illustration suggestions. The opportunity to create a trading relationship with another organization is not an inconvenience, like rainfall. It is a situation you should welcome – a situation you must be actively courting with intense activity. You need to be trade-ready. Being not-averse-to-fixing-something-up is just not good enough. No one is going to want to trade with someone who is making no effort to meet him halfway. You know how it works. Wallflowers don't get asked to dance.

ACORD users share and exchange data in order to do more business, and to do business better on behalf of their customers and stockholders. Different organizations, same data. Different goals, same data. Different value-add, same data.

I often talk about data as a payload. Data is the burden of messages, the freight carried in automated exchanges between systems and between businesses. Just like hard freight, data is more efficiently shipped when it is standardized. Think of containerized shipping, and the way it has transformed the global economy. Data standards bring the same benefits to business interoperability.

And just as the era of containerization has allowed globalized businesses to develop using the assumption of efficient, worldwide trans-shipping, so data standards enable a whole new era of business opportunity. At the fine-grained level, data standards are providing ease and reliability of data sharing and exchange between parties. But at a higher level, data standards provide a substrate for the development of enhanced businesses.

Just as businesses can now be created or adapted to take advantage of the infrastructure benefits of global standards such as currencies and containerization, so they can build on the

> **"Data is the burden of messages, the freight carried."**

basis of data standards. You want to shift your back-end costs to a more cost-effective region? Data standards let you do that. You want to hook your product up to a basket of complementary products in other markets or territories? Data standards let you do that. You want to embed your products and services in an array of contingent business areas that previously would have been too hard to connect with? Data standards let you do that.

These are all strategic, business-defining paths data standards make possible. They are not a "nice-to-have" but an existing reality in today's world. They are not secret capabilities revealed only to a few chosen mortals, but self-evident truths accessible to every business-minded person on the planet. It's out there. There's no unsaying it.

Isolation

Without standards, data items may be corrupted by system processes that were designed to make the data amenable to certain programs. In other words, data is used by some systems but not left in a state that makes it usable to other systems.

This was a reasonable approach to programming when systems lived in glorious isolation, and just getting a computer to reliably produce a desired behavior was a major triumph. We can see the implications of this approach in many legacy systems. The oldest data processing systems, such as those that process payroll or keep financial accounts, may manipulate and store data in ways that make perfect sense to themselves, but leave the data in an obscure or over-compacted form for other systems to use as input. This often happened because data storage was expensive in the early commercial computer systems. Programming languages were not always standardized, varying in dialect from generation to generation and platform to platform.

"Data was often compromised."

Data was often compromised to optimize existing hardware capabilities, and the notion of sharing data between systems was a dim dream in the minds of a few computer scientists.

Software engineering, being a relatively young profession, harbors side effects of early systems thinking beyond their practical business utility. While no IT professional today would shy away from standards that make her life easier, not all IT professionals recognize the fluidity of system-to-system collaboration. The modern business world dictates a thoroughgoing implementation of business standards in every project. The potential of erosion of data as it passes between systems that are not standards-aligned may not occur to individual engineering teams, because their responsibilities begin and end at the edge of their respective systems. All too often, there is no technical responsibility for the hazy space that floods the voids between our systems. This is the vacuum standards fill. And this is the zone where "the business" must assert its ownership over the data asset. In the spaces between our systems, and at their edges, business data standards perform the crucial functions of bullet-proofing, future-proofing and idiot-proofing the business's lifeblood: its information.

The exposed position of data in non-standardized environments gives the false impression all data is fragile. This is not so. When encased in recognized standards, data is tough, trustworthy and tractable.

Fragile Data

I believe the perception data is inherently fragile is a carry-over from our understandable desire to stress the human context in which data is used. And I am the first to agree data only has value in so far as it serves human interests and human goals. "Business" when it is used as an adjective, is often just another word for "human." We know businesses are made up of people, and that they exist to create value for people, perform services for people, and contribute to the satisfaction of people's needs. But it's all too easy to assume, therefore, any materials a business uses will be subject to human fallibility. "Computer error," right? Murphy's Law, right? Surely data is bound to be unstable if it's being handled and interpreted by fallible human beings. And so data standards somehow have no relevance.

This is the crux of the matter. Data standards are important precisely because they make data usable in contexts potentially compromised by normal human activities. This isn't such a peculiar idea. If your business centers on the manipulation of lumps of hot metal, you install the machinery needed to handle hot metal. At the very least, you issue your operatives with gloves. You build a methodology around the processing of an otherwise injurious material. You may inherit methods of working, and copy methods from other similar businesses. You will also look for new techniques and processes that will help you create your products more cost-effectively and distribute them more quickly to larger markets. Standards play a large part in this endeavor: standardized metallic compositions with known heat-retaining qualities, for example, and the standardized temperature scales themselves.

You Run a Data Business

If you run a data business — and everyone does, these days — your data is the raw material of the wealth you produce. Like most raw materials, it has the potential to be volatile, to "go off" or to become damaged during handling. But this doesn't mean we should shrug our shoulders and accept that level of risk. Water can destroy property and life, but we still manage to control it and distribute it across huge distances, with guaranteed quality and availability. Our civilization depends upon it. Standards are the way we manage data. They are the means of taming wild data. Data standards are containerization. They are commoditization. They are globalization. Standards form the basic business technology of the twenty-first century. They make modern business possible.

If you are struggling on without data standards, you are standing in a dangerous factory, awash with combustible, poisonous product. I wish I could make you smell it. In isolation, data resides in a dimension of clarity and purity. Outside of a standards-based environment it is a pernacious material to deal with — a treacherous, slippery, multi-headed beast. But it's no exaggeration to say this beast is leeching the life out of a slew of once-great businesses.

Are standards a panacea to this situation? Yes, they are.

Too great a claim to make? Not really. Get this: the problems of unstandardized data may be deadly, but the cure is simple. Think of unstandardized data as a mess of trip hazards. Standards sweep up those obstacles, pin them down. That wasn't so hard, was it? But you just saved a few lives.

Implementing standards isn't hard. Once you've done it, your business reaps the benefits for all time to come. Yes, you need to keep maintaining those standards; but I'd suggest you need to maintain your buildings regularly too. If you could see, touch and smell the decay that sets in within unstandardized data environments, and the corrosive knock-on effect to the value of the businesses harboring these environments, you'd be reaching for data standards with all the speed you could summon. It's part of my job to sense these conditions, and to help you sense them too.

19

The ROI Debate

How standards are paid for, and how they pay back

Did you know money has a shape? It does, and the insurance industry is one significant result of our realization of this fact of economic geometry. Money is a means of shifting value around time and space. Therefore how you choose to relate value, time and space describes a shape.

Here's an example. If you borrow $1 million with interest, you are pulling dollars from the future into the present. You're bringing money you'll have in the future into the present day. The interest you are charged is the fee for your time travelling.

If you lend someone $1 million, you're giving up present-day dollars and pushing them into the future (when your loan is repaid). The interest you receive is a reward for displacing your money in time.

Why is this important? Well, everything we do with money expresses a set of relationships between value, time and space. Every spending or saving decision we make has an impact on these variables. Every decision has a shape. However, to listen to some folks, the only shape in town is the one-off, case-related ROI model.

ACORD's experience with the development, roll-out and evolution of business standards is that standards describe a far different shape than the one usually associated with the standard ROI case. That hockey-stick graph you expect to see on an ROI case – it's not the only shape out there. In fact, while the hockey-stick graph is perhaps history's most predicted shape of money, it is the shape least often produced by real events.

In this chapter we look at where ROI applies, and where it doesn't. We tackle some ROI falsehoods. ROI isn't the only game in town, and it's dangerous to assume it is. I conclude by considering the risks of accidentally disinvesting from the standards movement – something a few organizations have tripped up on, to their detriment.

Under The Spell Of A Measure?

IT departments are coming under increasing pressure within businesses of all kinds, but in none more so than information intensive industries such as insurance. Computer systems have become a major component of delivering underwriting. As companies seek to reduce the costs of underwriting, they naturally seek to squeeze the budgets of underwriting's major components.

The instinctive restraint applied to IT spending is in one respect a reaction against expensive mistakes of the past, when businesses occasionally developed systems they didn't need. But in another important respect, the relative starving of IT budgets in recent years reflects business computing's coming-of-age. Systems are now accepted as part of the furniture. And, just like the furniture – and the people who sit on the furniture – systems have to justify their costs.

As business people, we justify our investments in many different ways. We sometimes hire people for whom we don't have an adequate existing job description, but because we know their talents and experience will add to our business capability. We sometimes run marketing campaigns in order to protect market share rather than to generate new business. We may open buildings in regions where we wish to make a general impression on the consumer's consciousness, despite the lack of an immediate market in that area.

In general, we combine hard and soft measures when we decide how we will direct our resources. We may prefer to base our decisions on hard measures, but we know the expansive and future-oriented dimensions of our businesses are those most likely to be driven by soft measures. The investments we make in growing and adapting our businesses are inherently risky. As insurance people, we should appreciate this more than many of our peers in other industries.

IT Spend

The problem is IT spending has become homogenised as a single type of activity, and moreover an activity purely allied to the "hard" side of the decision-maker's matrix. The first assumption is all IT spending is geared toward automating or improving existing business processes. The second, and associated, assumption is any resources we put toward automating or enhancing existing business processes can be measured in hard, dollar-saved, terms. That's why ROI is king. Return On Investment has become the only game in town.

ROI has its uses: and its uses are in decision-making areas governed by fixed boundaries and known comparators. These areas are somewhat rarer and more endangered than the rain forests.

The practice of building ROI cases is irrelevant to 90 percent of business, yet ROI is promoted as a tool throughout business, and especially in IT. But think about it: where is the relevance of ROI to these decisions:
• Should we launch a new product?
• Should we seek to take over a competitor?
• Should we build a new employee parking lot?

I guarantee in each of these generic cases, we could create convincing ROI cases that would greenlight or reject specific projects. (I also guarantee we could sculpt the earn-out portion of each case to influence

"The practice of building ROI cases is irrelevant to 90 percent of business."

the outcome according to our own preferences: but that's an argument for another day.) The point to notice about each of these decisions is ROI only has a role in their processing if we assume direct comparability between the start state and the end state. In other words, if our decisions are about altering the status quo but not replacing it, then ROI can be used to give us some sort of hard measure. In the first example, a new product will presumably capture a new market, so expected income can be offset against planned expenditure on developing and implementing the new product. Scenarios can be crafted around the desirability of a takeover in terms of access to new markets or reduction in per-customer costs. The parking lot decision is likely to revolve around existing employee costs and benefits.

Market Forces

But I submit, with or without the presence of an ROI case, decisions like these are taken on soft measures. Firms mostly develop new products because their competitors have done so. The key determinant in this decision is not ROI, but the potentially lethal consequences of a failure to respond. Many corporate takeovers are the result of market forces completely unconnected with business performance fundamentals. A fashion for mergers blows up in the market, and everybody is in play – whether they like it or not. Companies often acquire other companies simply to avoid being acquired themselves. And the parking lot? If you're growing your staff, and you have the land, then your lot will get bigger. Write an ROI case if you want – but you could also spend the time calculating how many angels can dance together on the head of a pin.

Notice the quantity missing from each of these decision areas is comparability between the start and end states. Business change is inextricably linked with forces controlling the organization's industry, markets and historical era. Business is a complex system. It's not possible to restrict the variables at play without parting company with reality. My experience strongly suggests the areas of business convivial to ROI case construction are shrinking rapidly, and are already in a stark minority.

I suspect most of us know ROI cases used to support decision making in the non-IT areas we have used here as examples are often provided to preserve a sense of scientific decorum, rather than to advance the efficiency or happiness of humankind in any way. But this shouldn't be the case for hard old IT, should it?

The plain truth is: today's IT projects are business projects like any other. The hard and fast, get-what-you-pay-for computer systems of the past have all been done. A faster way of cutting checks? It's been done – and the ROI was great, thank you very much. Better organization of enterprise information? Ditto. Cleaned-up customer data? Likewise.

What about a knowledge management system to support your helpdesk people? Is there an ROI to go along with that? It's possible to fix one up, and I've seen people work magic with the average length of problem fixes and their related costs. However, if your customer problem-solving capability is sub-standard, then you've got to fix it. Sure, you don't want to spend more than you need on fixing it. But you're going to fix it.

Decisions to invest in standards fall into the same category. Ask yourself this question: Is any modern business going to choose to stay outside the electronic trading community? You've got to do it.

ROI Potential Results from Adoption of Standards*

External Activities

Potential Cost Savings to:

Add one distribution channel 20%
Add one business partner/service provider 50%
Set up one new distributor 60%
Set up a proprietary interface 100%
License & appoint one agent 60%
Add one external system interface 30%

Internal Activities

Potential Cost Savings to:

Submit & quote one policy 20%
Underwrite a policy 20%
Process one claim 20%
Perform one policy service transaction 20%
Reinsure one policy 20%
Add one internal system interface 30%
Add one data dictionary/data models used internally 50%
Convert one non-standards-based system due to acquisitions 50%
Convert one standards-based system due to acquisitions 30%

* Based on average data from case studies shared with ACORD.

Patch Or Platform?

ACORD's roots are in improving the efficiency of inter-business data communications. We started life as an organization tasked with fighting the tide of paper. In those days, ACORD standards fit the classic ROI framework – no question about it. Pit electronic transfer against manual processing and electronic will win hands down, any day.

But that's been done. The key to ACORD's value today is not electronic trading per se, but systems collaboration built around standards. We've released data from its paper bearer, so that ROI case has been done. But in releasing data from its manual bonds, we have created a new world of interconnectivity. We've created a business environment in which systems can talk with each other with greater ease than ever before. We've enabled an entirely novel era of business-to-business capability.

Standards in our business began as a patch on a problem: a means of saving money in a repetitive, labor-intensive business process. They've now become a platform: a means of doing business.

The ROI case for enabling technologies such as ACORD's standards can in fact be stated. And the ROI case can be characterized in a very stark manner. The costs of adopting ACORD standards are the ACORD dues, plus the time and effort an organization must devote to implementing them. The returns are infinite.

How can I say this? It sounds crazy. But consider this: standards do not solve a problem for your business. *Standards reskill your business.*

Chinese Proverb

Give a man a fish and you feed him for a day. Teach a man to fish and you feed him for a lifetime.

Acquiring standards is the corporate equivalent of developing a new fundamental skill. Standards give the organization the ability to create new relationships and new lines of business in ways it has never had before. Standards are evolution for business. They're the next size up in brains.

We live and act in a complex world of multiple, interacting, fast-changing variables. Isolating a few of the more lumbering variables may allow you to build an ROI case. But what connection will that case have with the real world? We're better off acquiring the senses required to survive and thrive in the real world that's turned out around us.

Others Live by ROI

It's easy to believe ROI is the favorite decision making tool of business, or even the only decision-making tool available. I believe the energy given to discussing ROI is largely deceptive. ROI is one of those topics we can all appear to agree on. It's motherhood and apple pie. But it's not necessarily as influential as it appears. More people are talking about doing it than are doing it. And often they're talking about how *other people* are doing it.

For example, I frequently hear from colleagues in the insurance industry how the banks are solidly wedded to ROI as a principal tool of decision-making. Yet my contacts in banking tell me banks are increasingly dropping ROI as a procedure in IT projects. Banks see IT as a cost of doing business. There's no alternative to IT. So why waste time developing a case for doing something you've got to do? Decision-makers need to focus their brain cycles on implementing the right technology choices — not artificially considering whether they will or will not use technology.

There's a myth around that ROI forms the building blocks of every business apart from the ones represented in the room. But it's not so.

ROI Cases Don't Always Transfer

I often meet people who are searching for ROI cases they can apply to their business situations. We all want to learn from other people's successes — and, let's face it, avoid their mistakes. And we're all more than happy to find a short cut to the solution of a problem in our own backyard. If the answer to our problem is out there, let's have it!

We can share learning across projects and organizations. Indeed, ACORD's data standards embody shared learning. We can also share general lessons about implementing a technology or fixing a class of business problem. (That's why we go to school.) I think we all enjoy spotting patterns of success and failure in the project experiences we encounter: this is a natural way of extending our knowledge and testing our own powers of analysis. In fact, this is exactly the kind of learning exchange ACORD members enjoy as part of their involvement in the standards community.

However, I don't think any of these learning exchanges can be encapsulated and codified within an ROI case. ROI cases are not transferable. They are not architectures, not blueprints, and not reusable components. ROI isn't DNA.

> **"This is because an ROI case is a very specific route map."**

I could take a very fine ROI case from Company A, and wax lyrical about the benefits Company A had enjoyed as a result of its associated project. Unfortunately, this doesn't mean Company B will have the same results with the same ROI case, or even with an adaptation of the ROI case. This is because an ROI case is a very specific route map, devised for a very local situation and deployed at a time now passed. Those conditions are never going to be replicated. Do you really want an old weather report for some town that's a little like yours?

ROI Cases Not Proof

I've lost count of the number of times people have said to me: "You've got to prove standards will save us money."

I've thought about this in some depth, and I've come to the conclusion there are only two things I can comfortably prove about how money behaves in future time. The first is there's one surefire way to save money, and that's to stop trading. Companies that have gone out of business have admirably low spending profiles. The second maxim I can prove is there's one surefire way of getting more money, and that's to steal it from people.

A generic ROI case, offered as a solution to the random ills of all comers, is the nearest the modern business community has to snake oil. I won't listen to generic ROI cases. I'm not going to start peddling one myself.

> "A generic ROI case, is the nearest the modern business community has to snake oil."

I'd love to be able to prove standards will save you money. I'd love my every decision underwritten by some universal authority. I'd love to know every move I made in business was guaranteed to be successful and to produce some predetermined, quantified benefit. I'd love my business to run like a machine.

But then, presumably everybody would be smoking the same stuff. We'd all be running our businesses in our sleep, and somehow all coming out ahead. That doesn't sound right. That doesn't sound possible.

I can't prove speaking English will get you further than communicating with grunts and gestures. I can only point to all the folks who've taken up the language and are going places with it. I can't guarantee it won't be hard for you to learn the language. I can't guarantee you won't sometimes use the wrong words. I can't guarantee what you have to say has any value or will be heard with pleasure. I can only invite you to cross the language barrier and join those of us on this side: those of us who are making our way with it.

And I can put my hand on my heart and say the one true ROI is a false god. Don't elevate the ROI case to the status of an idol. ROI isn't a mathematical absolute, but a local example of arithmetic. ROI isn't a fundamental property of business, but a decision-making tool for local, circumscribed areas of activity.

Accidental Disinvestment: Don't Fall Off The Bus

Working-level relationships between members and ACORD tend to be deep and valuable. Business Analysts who contribute to ACORD groups or work with ACORD standards find the relationship rewarding and congenial. But all too often, these team members do not hold the organizational purse strings. They do not sign off their organization's ACORD dues. Often they do not realize their colleagues with budgetary responsibility may not have the same understanding of ACORD's value to the enterprise as they do.

ACORD is a community movement. It is a self-created grouping of insurance industry players who want to improve the economics, efficiency and effectiveness of the industry. As in any area of life, there are two ways the work can get done. The participants can do it themselves, or they can hire other people to do it for them. Neither route is "better." They both cost exactly the same.

In practice, ACORD is a combination of both funding routes. Members pay dues, but they also contribute their time and expertise. I make no bones over which component is the more valuable. The effort and experience of our members vastly outstrips the value of the dollars they pay in dues.

But dollars are visible, and time and expertise are not. Ben Franklin told us "Time is money" and you can almost hear him repeating that warning from the $100 bill where he lives on. Despite the simple truth that the involvement of its experts is an organization's real contribution to the ACORD community movement, massively outweighing its pure dollar contribution, it's the dues that have the highest visibility when it comes to making possible cuts in the organization's outgoings.

> **"ACORD is a community movement."**

ACORD is not a supplier. We don't sell products and we don't perform services. We are not a commodity, nor a brand. *We are an investment vehicle of the insurance industry.* We are an embodiment of pooled commitment to a better, more rewarding future for us all.

20

Thought Leadership

Are there geniuses amongst us whose powers of insight and superior intelligence mean they can effectively foretell the future for us? If someone could peer ahead with twenty-twenty foresight, then they'd save us all a lot of time, money and energy. I like to follow the predictions of experts, but only insofar as they inform current debates. I wouldn't want to place all my bets on the arguments of any one thought leader – though I might buy a position in a spread of them. But I guess that's the insurance professional in me speaking.

Resisting the future has a proud history. Some of the world's greatest minds have famously misread the future. Several years or centuries down the track, and blessed with twenty-twenty hindsight, we can shake our heads at their folly. But we have much to learn from their mistakes: not so much from the trends they failed to predict or the practices they believed would endure for ever, but the values they used to form their judgments.

Foretelling the Future

To start with, let's agree attempting to foretell the future is asking for trouble. "Among all the forms of mistake, prophecy is the most gratuitous."xxv Make a public bet about future developments and you invite scorn if your call turns out to be wrong. The praise you'll receive if your bet is correct will, by comparison, be somewhat faint.

So, why do people attempt to make broad statements about future events? I believe they do so because they wish to influence those future events. By saying such-and-such *will* be the case, they hope to set in motion or add their weight to the development they indicate. Similarly, those who warn about dire eventualities seek to influence our behaviors toward derailing those developments. Every pronouncement has its historical context. Predictions about the future of business or technology have the same status. No such prediction is untouched by the preferences of its maker.

Socrates

The finest example of a great mind miscalling the future of information technology is... Socrates. A great thinker and teacher, an intellectual leader, and one of the founders of western civilization, Socrates was vehemently opposed to the technology of writing. He believed the spread of writing would destroy the knowledge, culture and social fabric of the society around him. Writing, Socrates argued, removed people's need to remember things. It therefore destroyed their ability to reason. If people could simply look up facts and transmit ideas to each other via a written medium, they would no longer be involving themselves in the creation, storage, transmission and processing of information. He was horrified at the new technology's ability to deskill humanity and its potential to wipe out the glories of our oral culture and mental traditions.

> "Socrates was vehemently opposed to the technology of writing."

The first irony here is, were it not for the invention and dissemination of writing, we would never have heard of Socrates. His sayings (and "sayings" they are) come to us via writers, most notably Plato. Without this non-personal, automatic information technology, Socrates's thought leadership would have died along with his pupils — or possibly mutated, through the oral tradition, into a set of fairy stories.

The second irony, and the one with the most bearing on our own times, is writing caused an explosion in thought, invention, art and commerce. Writing did not kill off culture, but preserved its finest products and issued an invitation for all to enlarge the culture. Writing democratized mental labor. You no longer had to dedicate your life to remembering the relatively few known facts of the ancient world — a feat which presumably required excusal from tilling the fields or casting a net. You could read the wisdom of the ancients, and create the wisdom of the moderns.

It's odd, and perhaps charming, to think of a figurehead such as Socrates setting such store by the ability to memorize. The spread of computers through business in our lifetimes has freed us more and more from the bounds — and bonds — of our own memories. The availability of the Internet means we don't even have to schlep down to the library to look up a fact. Yet there are parents who worry (in a Socratic way, I guess) their kids' use of the net is robbing them of the "traditional skills" of research and discovery. We've already got a generation brought up on pocket calculators who can't make change at the electronic cash registers they work... But guess what? The small change is going anyway. Math isn't all arithmetic. And learning isn't all about looking stuff up in the most painful way possible. Acquiring and creating knowledge is a creative process, and computers are power tools that help the process. They don't replace the process, they just change it.

I feel slightly foolish trying to psychoanalyze Socrates, especially at this distance in time (and especially since he's in no position to pay a fee). But I'd guess what looks to us like pig-headedness, or perhaps nostalgia for tried and trusted methods, was in fact simply a failure to foresee the incredible enlargement of the field in which he toiled. We see this error repeated throughout history, and throughout modern business. It's a mistake we all make all the time.

Here are three reasonable statements about future developments that have all been made by people who knew what they were talking about. They all, tragically in some cases, misjudge the effects of scale. Doubtless you can think of other examples:

- The growth of the human population will outstrip the world's ability to feed it, leading to competition and suffering. (Thomas Malthus, 1798.)

- "the new mechanical wagon with the awful name – automobile"26 will never become universally used, because we'll never be able to train enough chauffeurs. (Unknown observer.)

- "I think there is a world market for maybe five computers." (Thomas Watson, chairman of IBM, 1943.)

Each of these statements takes a current situation, applies the prevailing logic of the situation to itself, and produces a future condition entirely consistent with known facts. But each excludes what could not possibly have been known by their creators: developments in different areas of human endeavor that unexpectedly crossed with the "home territory" of each expert.

Malthus

To take Malthus first: his math is undoubtedly correct. If food production increases linearly and population increases exponentially, then at some point the graphs cross and there are too many mouths to feed. However, we have been able to produce more and more food from fewer resources. We produce an incredible volume and variety of food, with a sharply reduced labor requirement. It's not a perfect picture, and famine is a real problem in many parts of the world. But the health problems of the western world now tend towards obesity rather than malnutrition, and the fastest growing medical problem in the southern hemisphere is expected to be depression.

Horseless Carriage

The triumph of the horseless carriage was achieved through a collection of world-changing forces, not least the rapid acceptance on the part of car owners they should also drive the machines themselves. In the United States we built our roads to catch up with automobile ownership. We developed chains of gas stations to serve the cars flooding on to the new blacktop ribbons. We oriented our cities around our roads. Our eating habits changed, as did our working lives. "Commuting" was originally the name given to buying a season ticket for the train into the city from an outlying town but became a nation-changing, car-based lifestyle. The error in the prediction car ownership would not spread was a belief in prevailing social attitudes. Few people realized the world was ready to remake itself in every financial, mechanical and geographical dimension to embrace the dream of unlimited personal mobility. But it happened. Look to China and you can see the same pattern repeating itself today.

Watson

Thomas Watson's famous prediction about the world market for computers is similarly based on his understanding of current behaviors. Watson was an excellent salesman and very well acquainted with the needs and plans of his company's customers. He did not foresee the democratization of computing. But even to use such a phrase in 1943 would have sounded crazy. It would have been like saying "the democratization of machine tools."

> My interest is in the future because I'm going to spend the rest of my life there. (Charles F. Kettering, engineer and inventor, 1876-1958.)

None of these wise folks could foretell how different strands in contemporary culture would cross, intermingle and create enlargements in existing markets. However their statements have sometimes acted unwittingly as goads to action. Charles Darwin was influenced by Malthus to develop his ideas of evolution according to processes of competition. Malthus also had a profound effect on economists and social reformers. The introduction of computers into corporations sparked demand for new types of application, undreamt of prior to their arrival. Henry Ford's organizational vision and leadership created the modern car industry, and arguably the modern world, in the teeth of "evidence" to the fact such a revolution could not take place.

I believe we'll always mis-figure issues of capacity. Our ancestors could not envision cities of the size we now have; but we have equal difficulty imagining the growing population centers of a century hence. Twenty years ago our best forecasters were predicting, by 2000, Americans would only need to work an average of 14 hours per week. We'd have run out of stuff to do, and we'd spend all our time relaxing. (Yeah, right.)

"Americans would only need to work an average of 14 hours per week."

When we do look for large-scale changes, we tend to look in the wrong places too — for all the best reasons. The oil was going to run out. Superbugs would bring a new global plague. But we keep wringing more productivity out of oil and finding new sources of the black gold. At the same time the energy companies are developing renewable resources — something that would be impossible without the investment capacity generated by the oil business and the demand for energy that is now integral to our society. We continue our war with disease: the enemies change, but the fight is relentless.

Doomsday Scenarios

We seem to love doomsday scenarios almost as much as steady-state ones. New York engulfed by a tidal wave? It's as likely/unlikely as McDonald's being around to open a branch on Mars. Rock-solid certainties can sometimes vaporize in front of our eyes — and the really surprising thing is we take such upheavals in our stride. I'm one of billions who grew up in a divided world, one apparently frozen in a standoff that might one day resolve itself through unimaginable violence and destruction. Then one day in 1989 that world fizzled away. We didn't go into shock: we got used to it.

I saw the same thing with the World Wide Web. Put the Web in front of someone for the first time, and for a few *seconds* they were delighted. But it was only seconds. We all assimilated this technology and its potential at an incredible speed.

And human beings have always adapted at lightening speed. Plant corn instead of chasing antelope? What, and throw away everything I know and hold dear? Okay. Stand at a lathe in a big shed instead of pushing a plow? What, just so me and my family can eat and live better? Sure. Wear a necktie and point at a PowerPoint show? Sounds good to me.

Leave everything I know and get in a leaky boat to go over the ocean and start a new life? Why not.

These are the kinds of hair-raising decisions human beings make, individually and in the mass, every day. We gamble with our lives. And, with perverse human logic, we gamble our lives to *improve* our lives. We throw away what we know, because we're not wedded to the devil we know.

We're more in love with the paradises we can imagine. In our heads, and in our hearts, the better futures we can imagine are just as compelling as the revealed facts of our present situation.

It may even be the "dumber" we are about our current situation, the easier we find it to embrace the future. We all know kids get on with new technology better than their parents' generation because they don't have a mass of prejudices to deal with. Socrates and his pals were against writing, but the merchants and administrators loved it because it immediately made their lives better. They weren't so worried about the direction of mankind, more concerned for the transactions of the day. By focusing on the here and now, they inadvertently created the future we inherited.

My analysis of the prophesying industry suggests strongly the more you invest your values in your predictions, the less likely you are to be right. Evolution doesn't follow a moral code. It's not listening to your values. It generates itself from a series of collisions, a mass of currents.

Predictions

I wish I knew the counterpart to this analysis: how we can make our predictions more accurate. All I can say is people tend to strive for the things that make their own lives more comfortable, pleasurable and exciting. This sadly means we want drugs as much as we want cars, and it means on average we act out of selfish reasons rather than altruistic ones. Bringing this home to the insurance industry, I think it means people will continue to seek products and services that minimize the uncertainty of life and reward loyalty and persistence. People will continue to attempt to master their personal fate, and they will do so through whatever means become available to them. If nanotechnology creates tiny machines that can go into the bloodstream and fix wayward cells, we'll line up to ingest the critters. If someone develops a suit of armor that makes people feel invincible in our cities, then we'll buy that. (The auto manufacturers tell us we've already bought it: it's called the SUV.)

On the business-to-business side, insurance will continue to develop via the proliferation of niche products. This is because a niche is simply a new type of risk or response to risk, and as long as humankind keeps developing we'll encounter new types of risk and invent new ways of mitigating them. And today's niche is tomorrow's mainstream. Many of us complain about niche products, because they're inherently complex. But maybe all this means is we don't want to learn something new. Maybe we're smart, like Socrates, and attached to the world we've learned how to dominate.

Ancient Greece is the birthplace of democracy and the information technology of writing, so feared by Socrates, proved to be the ultimate tool of democracy. Writing democratized thought, belief and commerce. Our contemporary information technology is further democratizing business by putting data, and the means to manipulate and share it, into the hands of the masses. The revolution created by the launch of the PC and then the opening up of the Internet continues to remake the world. The initial shock, and its stock market shadow, may have gone, but the legacy lives on. We've been constructing popular songs with the same limited set of notes for many generations now, and it doesn't seem like we're in danger of running out of new tunes. Artists keep finding new ways to paint bowls of fruit. It's going to be a long, long time before we exhaust the potential of this wave of information technology. The possibilities of combining and transforming information across organizations are, to all intents and purposes, as boundless as the stories yet to be written.

21

London Gets It

The world's oldest market becomes the newest – with standards

The progress being made in London (i.e. Reform) toward an open, highly efficient and flexible insurance market that confirms London's position as a leading world player is truly remarkable. There's a revolution underway in London, and its manifesto is standards. So I thought that I would share my thinking about ACORD's work in London and the market's role as a signpost to the future of the industry. And I trust that my comments will encourage you to develop a proactive strategy about standards in the London market, rather than having others do it for you and, more importantly, at your expense. In part, that is why ACORD was organized by the industry 35 years ago; to assemble practitioners with a stake in the business and a need to shape its future.

The Market is a Social Construct

London's insurance market started in the city's coffee houses more than 300 years ago. While much has changed in London and the world beyond in the intervening period, you'd be forgiven for thinking the only substantive change in the insurance community is its move from coffee houses to a plethora of pubs and wine bars. That's because, to its thousands of participants, the London market is above all a social construct. Business continues to be conducted face-to-face and personal relationships remain the bedrock of any career in the Lloyd's or company markets. The nurturing of ties beyond the trading floors is a key part of the day's activities and the social dimension is the core of London's success, past and future.

> **"Personal relationships remain the bedrock."**

Digital Networks Do Not Challenge Human Networks

Electronic systems seem, on the face of it, to challenge this situation. The introduction of systems designed to facilitate transactions amongst parties (rather than, say, to store records of customers) appears as an especial insult to this human network. Traditionalists shake their heads and condemn such systems as attempts to destroy the special qualities of the market: to deny the human factors that make it the greatest place on the planet to do insurance business, and to denude it of its greatest capability – that of accepting every risk brought before it.

The defenses mounted by traditionalists from inside the market run up against equally extreme condemnations from outsiders. Systems professionals from other industries, and experts from the banking sector in particular, look at the legions of brokers striding through London's narrow streets weighed down by paper files and are dismayed at the antiquated, expensive and time-consuming processes the market's reliance on manual systems implies.

In most cases these external critics have seen the labor-intensive elements of their own industries junked without much sentimentality. Their open-outcry traders have gone, their back and front offices are integrated for "straight-through processing" and staff has been removed in ever increasing numbers from the deal-making activities. At the same time resourcing has shifted to customer service in the pursuit of greater customer loyalty and increased lifetime value from customers.

> **"Outsiders see nothing but fat waiting for the overdue butcher knife."**

In the majority of business sectors these days, the "relationships" we pursue and invest in with the most effort are with customers, not with partners in the supply chain – who, in any case, relate to each other as customers. So managers in non-insurance financial services often look at the London insurance and see nothing but fat, waiting for an overdue butcher knife.

One of the difficulties outsiders sometimes have when getting to grips with the London market is their expectations of the word "market" itself. In most contexts, and especially the business contexts that have promoted the growth of online business-to-business exchanges over the last several years, a market is a simple machine that brings buyers and sellers together around the shared concept of value.

Not a Commodity But Not Always Unique

ACORD has something to offer reformers and traditionalists alike. And although we are recent arrivals in our own right with an office at the London Underwriting Centre, we have been working with industry organizations (some now gone) in this market for many years. And as I continue to meet and talk with London players, getting the measure of their aspirations and constraints, I find the match between ACORD's mission and London's emerging future growing

> **"ACORD has something to offer reformers and traditionalists alike."**

stronger and stronger. It's not that the defenders of tradition are wrong and the techno-snipers are right. There is a huge amount in the London market's makeup and experience that does make it a truly unique place to do business. And there is massive value in the human network it represents. But these truths – the legacy of everything London's been doing right for three centuries – are in no way incompatible with standards, collaborative systems, and improved efficiencies. Technology does not have to be a blunt weapon.

Value is often encapsulated in prices but it can also be expressed through banded negotiations (better known as "haggling"). When investors

> **"Technology does not have to be a blunt weapon."**

analyze the state of a securities market, they know all the information they need to assess a stock or basket of stocks is "in the market," expressed in the listed prices buyers are prepared to pay at any given moment. The information that makes up this kind of market is beautiful in its simplicity: the name of what's for sale, and how much it costs. These are two data items any straightforward market can agree on readily. In fact, the need to stabilize these two elements of trade is at the root of the basic human efforts at standardization: written language, weights and measures, and currency.

However, the London market is not a commodity market. It's not a place where anonymous people gather to exchange value based on a shared understanding of simple public information. In fact, it's precisely the reverse situation. People who know each other very well – who trade and often socialize with each other all their lives – come together to make deals around unknowns. Their market is in risks the world has never seen before, and does not know how to price. These risks are not commodities that can be traded anonymously: you need to know what you're doing, for one thing, and you need deep pockets for another. The simple information outsiders assume defines a market is absent in London.

The lack of a simplifying, encapsulating mechanism such as price tends to support the insider's argument that the London market is "different," and not susceptible to improvements from automation, let alone standards-based collaborative systems. If every deal in the market is unique, then what role do standards have?

Accuracy Trumps Price

The fact of the matter is, however, that not ever deal in London is a one-off. There's more repetition than may be immediately apparent. Furthermore, even the most exotic deals share certain common elements with other deals. Most importantly, the lack of a simple price mechanism to take centre stage in the electronic arena actually masks a more significant, and indeed acute, need for standards in the London market. The continued operation of the market, and its growth, depends vitally on the exchange of information. The value of correct information exchange in insurance markets is, I believe, potentially more significant than the value of correct prices in commodity (financial) markets. Why? Because, as many have pointed out, the insurance market is about promises, not products. And promises have the potential to burn the future.

"Not every deal is a one-off."

"The insurance market is about promises, not products."

Look at it this way: If you buy a commodity at the wrong price, you have a theoretical loss or profit. Since prices change in the market in line with the waxing and waning of supply and demand, there is every chance for you to reverse your profit or loss at another trading opportunity.

Consider what happens if you make an insurance deal and the information about the deal is not correctly captured and transferred to each party in the deal. Since insurance deals are about the future, there's a period where this doesn't seem to matter —

"When the gentleman in the red robe used to ring the bell, players scrambled for their seats."

at least, not to those individuals who have executed the deal. But then what happens when the risk crosses the line from potential to actual? When the ship sinks, or the satellite falls out of the sky?

At the Lloyd's building in London, a gentleman in a red robe rings a bell when such an eventuality occurs. I guess this is when the music stops and the players metaphorically scramble for a seat. If it turns out the information you collected about the insurance of this risk is incomplete, missing or — perhaps worst of all — held in different versions by the signatory parties, then there's no seat for you.

Critics Wide Off the Mark But London Gets It

Surprisingly, the efficient and effective collection, storage and exchange of risk-related information has not, until comparatively recently, been near the top of the agenda of most London market players. The Reform Movement has risen in prominence because of changes in the market's environment. The key factors are:

• Increased pressure from government and its regulatory bodies to create more transparency and audit ability in the industry following well-publicized losses in the 1990s

• Increased ownership of market players by multi-sector financial organizations who cannot treat the capital they deploy in the insurance market any differently than the capital they utilize elsewhere

• Increased competition from other markets, notably Bermuda, that have not been so squeamish about adopting reforms to allow themselves to write more business in a wider field of risk.

External critics who imagine there is a price mechanism buried somewhere in the London market that needs liberating so new opportunities may flourish are wide off the mark. Such critics would be better looking to the execution records of their own markets and musing on the fact London is so cavalier with its own equivalents. To put some measure on this, it takes an average of 154 days for a policy to be issued once the deal is struck. The gap between seeking settlement and a claim being made is a comparatively speedy 42 days.[27] It seems the rest of the business world may be "always-on," but the London insurance market is pretty much on "standby."

Insiders often remark that these figures, while apparently poor, do not really matter. Some regard the issue of contract certainty – that parties know what they've signed up to – as a piece of politically correct window-dressing mounted to mollify the politicians and the pundits. Not every risk yields a claim, obviously. So the majority of deals age and die without their terms ever being examined. When a poorly understood deal is called to account, why the lawyers can argue it out. Isn't that what lawyers are for?

Dr. Jekyll and Mr. Hyde

There's a sly logic operating here – a logic that goes with the nudge and wink of a face-to-face, relationship-intensive trading culture. But this reasoning is faulty business practice. We are entrusted with large sums of other people's money. Have we covered a risk, or not? These questions must have answers. And how can we continue to win the business of an increasingly corporate and global customer base? The value of trust, much lauded in the London market, is betrayed by the market's historically laissez-faire attitude to capturing and exchanging core information.

Let me say I understand how these misperceptions arise, and how they can be ramified in a close-knit community. Perspective isn't always easy to get right, particularly when you're down amongst what some executives call the "muck and bullets" of daily business. But London is not a lost cause; far from it. London has woken to the extreme danger of its stance on information issues and is taking actions to ensure its future success, and to achieve a quantum leap in performance, size and value over the coming years. In fact, when it comes to the successful use of standards, I believe London is showing the rest of the insurance community the

"London is showing the way ahead."

way ahead. London gets it. And London can advance the digital revolution throughout the industry.

Daily Habits Define Markets

What goes around comes around. Industries with long pedigrees evolve but they also develop cyclical patterns. For those of us in the midst of an industry's workings, it can naturally seem that the grooves created by daily habit define the market in every aspect and that any overall forward motion doesn't exist. So we habituate ourselves to the transactions and traditions in our midst and slowly become numb to larger developments in our environment.

"How about we use my tennis balls?"

The London insurance market occupies less than a square mile of real estate. When I observe the market in operation, it reminds me of a solar system. The various parties revolve around each other in a set of seemingly fixed relationships. If you want to be part of this stately dance of planets, you have to choose an object and live with its orbit.

We also no longer accept isolation on our home planet, but send probes to the other bodies in our neighborhood and peer to the very edges of the universe. There are, similarly, seers and doers in the London market who do not accept the tracks laid down by tradition are necessarily the only paths the market may take. These good people are explorers, pioneers – practical folks. Unfortunately, these reformers bang up against what we'll have to call astrologers: people who find human meanings amongst the patterns of their environment.

> **"Seers and doers in the London market do not accept the tracks laid down by tradition."**

Superstition is an incredibly strong force in its own right. There is, for example, a recurring belief that the alignment of the solar system's planets will create some kind of catastrophe on earth. Doomsayers have long held that whenever the planets form a line that includes the earth, tidal waves and earthquakes will be unleashed. A popular book published in 1974 predicted an alignment in 1982 would destroy Los Angeles. The fear of alignment-generated disasters reappears in the media every few years, making it a kind of comet of the news system.

Common Fears and Foggy Notions

"Simplifying pathways gives everyone more mobility, more latitude."

I think it's possible to detect the symptoms of planetary- alignment-style superstition. Think about it: the (by-now) traditional model of a modern, efficient, systemized industry takes each significant type of player and threads them on a line. The parties are, in more ways than one, online. Surely this kind of geometry will produce some terrible kind of effect. Well, I believe the common fears about planetary alignment are to do with foggy notions of how gravity works. And I submit that fears about introducing efficiencies into the London market – connecting people up in shorter, straighter lines – tap into vague but scary beliefs about how capital works. My evidence? When they reformed the stock market in London in the mid-80s, they called it "Big Bang."

Let's be clear. Simplifying any of the pathways amongst the parties of the London market will not cause a meltdown. Creating greater connectivity will not result in a massive rush of capital to a single player. It'll simply free the players from the time-honored paths currently composing their repertoire. It'll give everyone more mobility, more latitude.

The Slingshot Effect

There's something else about planetary alignment that may be helpful to our cause. There *are* indeed relationships amongst the planets that can deliver exceptional power to human beings – sometimes once-in-a-lifetime opportunities. These relationships are not so easy to discern as accidental straight lines, nor do they have the same simple aesthetic appeal.

NASA scientists can model the motions of the planets to determine optimum launch dates for spacecraft, giving each craft the most energy-efficient route to its destination. The scientists exploit the "slingshot effect" of a planet's gravity. If you wander near the right planet at the right time, you can use its orbit to whip you onwards to your next rendezvous. Modelers can plot apparently devious courses through the solar system that send probes whizzing like pinballs in the fastest and cheapest courses to their goals.

London's embrace of standards gives the London market *as an entity* its own slingshot power. The adoption of global standards gives the entire market a layer of accessibility and efficiency that will advance it far beyond its competitors as a venue for conducting insurance business.

> **"Standards give the entire market a layer of accessibility."**

The Curse of a Polarized Vision

Technology has vaporized a slew of traditional markets, recreated them in the ether and left their former halls empty. So the advent of enhanced connectivity in the London market has tended to create a polarized vision of the future as being an abrupt fork in the path. The vision comes down to this: Is our business best conducted on the floor, or in the air? This kind of binary thinking is wrong.

The role of technology is not to destroy business practice, but to liberate it. The physical structure of a market floor, together with its stations or pits and its accepted etiquette for making transactions,

> **"Technology's role is not to destroy business practice but to liberate it."**

form in themselves a technology. It's not computer technology, but it is technology: the technology of human communications. Before the telegraph and the telephone, this is how all business was done. Buildings keep the rain off and non-players out. Guilds, companies and charters guard the probity and capitalization of participants. Good manners and local jargon are the communications protocols used by the players.

It's More About *Communicating* Than Processing

The technology of interconnected computers does not represent a wholesale demolition of this traditional model, any more than a new method of building construction threatened earlier markets. Just because a building can be built higher or larger or with more flexible accommodation than before does not mean the business conducted within the building disappears. Indeed, business is only enhanced by new methods of construction. That's *why* new building technologies are created. Look at the skyline in EC3.

"My data system isn't speaking to your data system."

Similarly, computers let organizations store and exploit information resources more effectively than the manual processes they replace. Where standards bear down on the evolution of markets is the level of communications protocols: the ways in which people deal with each other. These are the most personal components of the "existing system" of the market, and therefore the components people grow most affectionate towards. What we do every day seems to be who we are. How can we sacrifice such a human quality to a machine?

It's worth noting that the sacred place of humans in the market's business is not a view shared equally by everyone involved. One player told me: "The London market is people-centric and there is much invested in the chain. The people on the street see themselves as the delivery mechanism. But their managers see them more as facilitators."

"Put the focus on opportunities that truly deserve the attention of humans."

In any case, the use of business standards does not entail the destruction of human interaction. Far from it. Adopting ACORD industry standards makes for more valuable human interactions demanding more creativity, more subtlety, more negotiation, and more profit. Using ACORD standards lets us allocate our time and energies to the opportunities that truly deserve the attention of humans. We consign the humdrum – "business as usual" – to an automated layer and elevate the cream – "business as unusual" – to pride of place in the human realm.

Most rational people are prepared to buy this argument in principle. But they balk at drawing the line between standard and non-standard information items. And then they don't use standards at all. They're right to balk at drawing the line. Where they're missing a trick is in assuming if they can't draw the line once and for

"Standards: apply them a little or a lot."

all time, then standards can't help them. Business information or data standards such as ACORD's are designed specifically to work as a spectrum. You can apply them a lot, or a little. You can modify the extent to which you use the standards depending on situation and circumstances. The standards do not force-fit your business. They offer you a range of componentized, market-tested, and industry-agreed upon vehicles for exchanging information. It's up to you how much you ride, and how much you walk.

> **"The development of data standards is an incremental affair."**

ACORD Is Animated By the Market

The London International Financial and Options Exchange is one example of how standards and electronic markets have developed and suggest implications for insurance industry reform. Other markets followed their lead and the open architecture created opportunities for market players rather than restricting their options.

These are issues we have met and dealt with many times in ACORD's history, and undoubtedly we will do so again. But the development of data standards is an incremental affair, involving the serial production of versions that keep up with the development of business in the real world. If I believed a standard froze for all time the ways an industry could function, then I would not be doing what I do every day. ACORD standards progress through a managed process of alignment so they best express the objects relevant to the business they serve.

> **"ACORD is organized as a function of the market, animated by market players and answerable to them."**

That's why it's so important that the developments "in the air" of the market make it to the standards development process. ACORD is organized as a function of the market, animated by market players and answerable to them. This is so the standards are designed, packaged and distributed in faithful service of the industry that gave us birth. As the market changes, we modify the standards to meet those challenges head-on.

Using automated systems can clearly help companies succeed — there's no doubt about that. But systems can also bring organizations to their knees. That's also a sad fact of life. The truth for most

> **"ACORD encapsulates business intelligence in its standards."**

companies is that judicious use of systems allows them to score massive efficiencies in their "business-as-usual" lines and free up resources to develop their "business-as-unusual" lines. They give themselves more headroom and more brainpower to focus on the cream in the business.

> **"A data standard isn't a shopping list; it is a description of market behavior."**

Data standards allow us to work together using "highest common factors" rather than "lowest common denominators." That's why ACORD standards-setting is a member-driven process. We're encapsulating intelligence in our standards, so that those adopting the standards can get the biggest benefit from the standards they deploy.

This is the way information intensive industries evolve. Industries that are growing commoditize today's high-value, one-off deals into tomorrow's business-as-usual as they garner experience in those deals. Skimming and canning today's cream creates more space for new high-value niches to take root and grow. If you don't standardize in this way, you only starve out new opportunities. So this is what successful businesses have always done. It's just that it all happens much faster these days.

Both Niches and Commodities

Capitalism is a force of creative destruction. New business thrives in the spaces cleared of old business, much as forests burst to life after fires. (In fact, fire is the earliest form of agricultural management.) What makes the London market's cream so special it can't be canned? Cream-canning in other industries often takes the form of simplifying and packaging a complex product. But many market participants believe the business transacted on the London market is too complex to be treated to such harsh industrial processes. It's as though the atomic bonds of each deal would dissolve in the stress of homogenization.

This is where the perspective of the data specialist is so helpful. As experienced modelers of data — it's what we do all day — we at ACORD are expert in creating standards that preserve the variations, ranges, nuances and interrelationships of data. A data standard isn't a shopping list. It's a description of a set of attributes and relationships that work together to convey information of importance to the business domain it serves. We faithfully reflect the actual information content and context of the information in the market. The data model we build is a working model: pump real data items into it, and it will behave as the market does. Our aim is to discover and enact the standards inherent within the market's information and behavior, not enforce some simplistic pattern on the market. We are concerned to clarify and enable rather than simplify and limit.

Commonality Amidst the Complexity

I am the first to agree the payload of insurance industry messages is more complex than that of commoditized financial services such as retail banking. However, amidst the complexity there is commonality. We aim to carry the commonly definable portions of insurance industry data so that data owners can give more attention to their unique data. (And for their unique data, we make provision in the standards for that too.)

It's beholden on us as industry players to discover which parts of our payloads can be part of a data standard. I maintain the proportion of the information model we all hold in common is quite high, and getting higher every day as we develop our standards still further. But I don't believe in enforcing my view of the dividing line (between common and unique) on anybody else. We make as much available in our standards as possible, so that our many diverse users can determine for themselves where they draw the line without any of them being constrained by an artificial ceiling.

This all encompassing scope presents us with the need to balance a comprehensive dictionary with implementation guides and tools that can effectively apply a subset of that dictionary to meet specific business needs. In general, trading parties need to reduce the status of information types that appear unique by virtue of the genuine exotics to which they cling.

The 80:20 Rule

So we need to make enthusiastic use of the 80:20 rule, or the Pareto Principle as it's also known. And the great thing about the 80:20 rule is that it can be applied recursively. That means, once you've drawn a dividing line between your exotic and common items, you can draw another one

"ACORD standards in today's IT networks improve your game."

across the divided parts. Also, let's bear in mind that the 80:20 rule doesn't mean you necessarily draw a line at the 80 per cent mark. Your Pareto line may come in anywhere on the scale. It doesn't really matter where it falls, so long as it does fall.

Ironically, one of the clearest systemic problems in the London market is the too-tight binding of data items in traditional, standardized packages. Since these packages use the technology of paper, their inflexibility and constraining effect is apparently invisible. ACORD data standards coupled with today's networks have an enormous transforming power and you can see how choosing to adopt data standards in your organization's IT strategy raises the game any player plays.

"Turn wires into business pathways."

ACORD Is Not a Technology Organization

Standards are a means of an industry combining and collaborating around better ways of working. That's why ACORD is a nonprofit (industry funded) membership organization, and why we are not aligned with any regulator, or technology vendor, or other external influence. Standards formally capture the structure of the information the industry, as a body of interested parties, needs to transact, transform, share and audit.

ACORD is not a technology organization, but a business effectiveness organization that enables the best use of information technology. ACORD standards are an expression of the community's urge to grow. Connectivity – in the form of fixed and wireless networks, and the plethora of devices and systems that can be attached to them – creates the potential for novel forms of commercial collaboration, product and service delivery and indeed product and service design. But physical connectivity is only a *potential* benefit. We need to turn wires into business pathways. And this is a huge part of ACORD's role. Data standards deliver internal efficiencies, but they have even greater value in opening up new pathways to commercial creativity – on a global scale.

"Standards encapsulate the DNA of the business."

The business and IT dividing line has shifted and the line has become increasingly blurred. Business folks are now computer literate and are now extremely well equipped to articulate their requirements of technology. Similarly, IT folks are now more business-savvy, and during the 1990s saw their industry lead the business community in terms of financial, construction and delivery innovation. As the waves of evolution sweep back and forth along the beach, the line in the sand is washed away each time. It's time we stopped pretending we need that line.

Standards are the single most important vehicle in the removal of the old dividing line between the business and IT. Standards such as ACORD's encapsulate the DNA of the business and make it available to IT systems. And standards are developed, governed and transmitted by dedicated professionals from the businesses they serve.

> **"The old walls have tumbled and an infinite number of new relationships have become possible."**

Those Who Succeed Focus on the Information

ACORD bridges the artificial business and IT divide and gives contemporary technology and business practice a much wider scale. Boundaries are falling wherever we look. Bank customers drive their own bank accounts via the PC. Supermarket customers instruct the entire grocery supply chain to deliver the weekly food order to their door. Companies construct and dissolve working alliances around the world and around the clock, using the power of the network to link resources with a flexibility and efficiency we could not dream of even ten years ago. The old walls have tumbled and an infinite number of new relationships have become possible. ACORD standards enable organizations to discount the boundaries that have traditionally constrained their ambitions, and to exploit the possibilities of a world that's now effectively open for business.

I believe information technology is an engine of business evolution. Harnessing this engine is down to mindset. Those who succeed with information technology do so because they focus on the "information" part, not the "technology" part. They have the resolve to articulate their strategies, communicate with their partners, and influence the environment within which they operate. And this is

> **"Business now bleeds over the boundaries of organizations."**

exactly what ACORD does. We articulate the current and future needs of the community, express those findings in a way that's accessible to people and systems alike, and release our deliverables into the world to add enduring bottom-line value.

The Business Boundaries

Some business writers have expressed the opinion that IT doesn't need creative management. In their view, IT is a cost of doing business and shouldn't be privileged above any other business function. And I agree. Technology isn't the point. But business information – that's the wealth of the enterprise. You shouldn't have to care too much about boxes and wires. But information – the lifeblood of your business – you'd better care about that! If you don't care, you won't exist. Information is vital. You create it, acquire it, aggregate it, process it and trade it. If you're not managing those activities carefully, you're not in business: you're going out of business.

In the days when information was just a concern limited to the organization's own administrative domain, the efficiency and effectiveness of information management were not highly visible measures. But today, business bleeds over the boundaries of organizations. We work together on behalf of our clients. We exchange information with each other, and create new opportunities together. Being an isolated player simply isn't an option any more. The rules have changed. Today's insurance industry is precisely about connectivity, because it's concerned with creating new offers that mobilize wider sets of expert players and reach deeper into markets. The industry is competitive, sure: but it's also cooperative.

> "Without standards, managers aren't managing: they're praying."

Business information standards are the single most important issue in contemporary management. Without standards, there's no genuine connectivity, there's just spaghetti. Without standards, there's no transparency to your business processes, just shadows where error and fraud can breed. Without standards, managers aren't managing: they're praying.

The business information revolution is upon us. It's a revolution of our own making, a product of our own collective will. Business wants business to be better: to be more profitable, more accountable and more creative. Information is the precious resource that is driving our progress and the confident, careful management of this resource through its lifecycle sorts the winners from the losers. And in our highly connected world, membership of the standards-using community has become the ticket to the game. In the end, if you're not going to use standards, then you're gone. The future unfolding around us is one of immense opportunity.

A Future-Proof Strategy is Essential

Regardless the size of your firm, making provision in your plans and strategy for industry standards is important. You can always determine the scale and level of industry participation, but factoring in what your trading partners are doing should be on your radar screen. You want to avoid hitting a brick wall someday for not have considered issues that transcend the boundaries of your organization.

Like a London cabbie, you need to know where you're going and the best route. You also need to observe the traffic flow, congestion charges and detours along the way. And you cannot delegate such responsibility to a trading partner or supplier in the hope that they will always know what is in the best interest of your firm. Doing so may become an extremely expensive ride. But unlike a taxi, there is no visible meter serving as a constant reminder of your lack of information and planning. Someone in your firm who is responsible for operations, information infrastructure and workflow must have the "Knowledge." And a team of a few people would be even better.

"I see London moving forward at a rapid pace."

ACORD has been leading the way toward ever more reliable, value-adding and opportunity-creating information exchange for 35 years and we are proud to offer our companionship for the journey ahead. A few may marginalize London as a unique but small player in a global marketplace. I see London moving forward at a rapid pace. I see it clarifying its business process, releasing its expertise and accelerating the development of the oldest insurance market into a bright example of secure, transparent and profitable trading. And ACORD will be an integral part of that transformation.

"I understand, Raeburn, you've had some trouble mining our legacy systems."

22

The Beginning

The movement for moving information

ACORD is now more than three decades old. As a thirty something, the organization has seen its share of business cycles, and business fashions. But throughout these decades of change, we have remained true to our primary mission. We're here to reduce complexity and enlarge opportunities for insurance industry players. We started out doing just that with paper forms, and now we do it with XML. As the future unfolds, ACORD members will continue to wring costs out of our industry's processes and broaden the industry's scope for competition and collaboration, whatever surprises technology may have for us down the pike. We'll continue to center our value-add around the concept of inviolable data, of data as an asset, of data as the asset of contemporary business.

It's easy to be skeptical when politicians and business leaders reach for "the vision thing." Sometimes you can't help getting the feeling they're reading from a script prepared by "spin doctors," and that in real life they'd run a mile from any touchy-feely sentiments about what's best for the business environment. But ACORD is not a political or a commercial entity. There is no percentage in my painting a grand picture that doesn't agree with the reality of what we're trying to do. ACORD does not have hidden agendas. We're simply an expression, a formalization if you will, of the industry's need to agree on collaborative standards to save us all time and money while creating a foundation for business innovation. Our "vision thing" is but the focal point of the industry's ambitions. ACORD is the place where those lines of vision meet.

That's why I think of ACORD not as a not-for-profit organization (though it is one), not as an industry standards body (though it is one), not as a center of excellence in business collaboration (though it is one); but as a cause.

Improving the Business

ACORD is an organized project tasked with improving the business environment. It's every bit as much a cause as the cause of democracy, or equality, or education. And these high ideals project into today's business space with renewed urgency. The struggle to introduce transparency into business management in the wake of corporate scandals is one expression of the general cause of higher ethical standards in business. ACORD's continued mission to develop, implement and promote standards throughout the insurance industry, and to act as a beacon for other industries, is part of a wider, and widely shared, quest for better, smarter, sharper business management.

"It is a struggle to introduce transparency into business management."

Our cause includes the elimination of wasted effort, but also the encouragement of innovation. Our cause promotes standards as a platform for creativity: standardization as a means of differentiation. Our cause addresses the internal processes of organizations, helping them return value to their stakeholders rather than watching dollars seep into the sand. Our cause addresses the meeting points between business partners, helping collaborators work together more efficiently, and giving them the means to extend their product and service offerings.

A Healthcare Regime

ACORD's cause is somewhat like a healthcare regime. Call it a business healthcare policy. Like the best healthcare approaches, ACORD's work supports three key areas of business life: maintenance, development, and recovery. Some businesses pay too little attention to their healthcare, and consequently spend much of their time in recovery mode. They're hit by disasters. They are not in control of their own destinies. They fall prey to whatever is "going around." But just like people who seek a pill for every ill, businesses that ignore the other areas of healthcare are opting for a lower quality of life, and possibly for a shortened lifespan. Businesses need to look after their existing capabilities, and extend them, not just rush to replace parts that fail. Businesses also need to be reaching for new ways of doing business, and new places to do business, not just repeating the behaviors that served them well in the past. ACORD's standards, and its standards-building process, provide a vital way for businesses to maintain, extend and repair themselves. That's why ACORD is a sensible insurance policy in its own right.

> **"Businesses also need to be reaching for new ways of doing business."**

A Movement

So I want you to be prepared to hear about ACORD's cause when you interact with our people. And I want you to recognize your part in the standards movement. I know you already support our work, and you want to help spread its adoption. I salute you for all you are doing for the standards movement, a movement which is ultimately far greater than any of us involved in it, even those of us privileged to speak in its behalf. It's time we held our heads up, and showed our pride in what we have achieved as a collective, self-supporting, self-directing body.

ACORD members represent the industry leadership and as such have changed the face of their industry. And they have done so without pump-priming from any government or interest group. They have crafted and deployed standards in a myriad of different business situations, and proved their business value-add, without the dubious benefits of spin or deep-pocketed sponsors.

> **"ACORD members have changed the face of their industry."**

Our standards have evolved free of the influence of monopolies, and remained untied to specific technologies, despite the lure of siren voices. We have been open, transparent, honest and inclusive in all we have done. I believe that's an achievement we can be proud of as we continue to nurture the progress of standards, and help to make our great businesses so much greater.

23

ACORD – The History

Throughout all the changes in our industry, and the expansion of our work over thirty-five years to encompass every aspect of the insurance business, our reason for existing, and our value-add, has orbited around the relationship between different parties. ACORD's outputs – its products, if you will – are standards. But the mission those standards fulfill is the removal of duplication, misunderstanding, delay, cost and commercial constraint amongst the players in our industry. This means our standards, and our standards-setting process, enable connections amongst many types of parties. We're an every-to-every connector, a universal adapter, a meeting-place, a co-operatively owned factory producing tools to enable businesses to work together with efficiency and effectiveness.

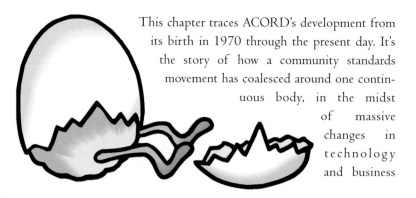

This chapter traces ACORD's development from its birth in 1970 through the present day. It's the story of how a community standards movement has coalesced around one continuous body, in the midst of massive changes in technology and business practice. It's also a story of committed people, working together to create a better business environment, attempting to read the future, and keeping true to the needs of their sponsoring organizations and their customers.

You'll notice a pattern emerging in this brief history. Put simply, standards initiatives emerge in business areas experiencing acute pain through duplication of work and an inability to share information efficiently. As those initiatives begin to deliver, the responsibility to promote and develop them begins to overwhelm the groups who gave birth to them. At the same time, initial responses to proposed standards inevitably reveal interested parties who weren't included in the original work of the group. It's a fundamental characteristic of standards that they reach out to wider populations, who – if the work is relevant and competent – will start to identify where their own needs have been omitted. Before you know it, a small, local initiative has become the topic of global inquiry and competing goals. It's at this point the originating group typically seeks help from a standards organization whose only responsibility is standards, and whose competences are solely dedicated to producing and promulgating standards.

ACORD has therefore grown incrementally, its useful gravity attracting smaller bodies. This is a matter of physics, not predatoriness. Standards are the procedural equivalent of economies of scale. Just as a company can lower the unit cost of production by concentrating manufacture in a plant, so a company can lower the costs of its information management by using standards. And ACORD is, of course, a not-for-profit body.

ACORD's values are conveniently summed up in the Concise Oxford Dictionary's definitions of "accord":

> 1. consent, mutual agreement... 2. treaty of peace; harmonious correspondence in color, pitch, tone, etc. 3. volition (*of one's own accord*).

We're happy to co-opt these meanings, even if we are "missing" a C. And did you notice that "a cord" is a means of threading things together, and is usually made up of many strands twisted together for strength...?

Participation

ACORD was conceived by independent insurance agents. Agents operate in a web-like network of complex relationships. The network is their natural environment, and they have lived with the realities of networked business for much longer than other types of business who have come to discover their interdependencies through the spread of technology. Agents have long known moving information is a major factor in providing good service, containing costs and expanding revenues. As intermediaries in the middle of the workflow, they were the first and best emissaries for the standardization cause.

> "Moving information is a major factor in providing good service."

And it all began with the IIAA (Independent Insurance Agents Association) of California and the committee they organized in 1970, known as the Agency-Company Operations Study Committee. The committee's remit was to assemble a group of insurers and agencies to discuss how they could together reduce the cost of doing business in the American Agency System. Interest in this mission grew nationally, and responsibility for the project soon passed to the NAIA (National Association of Insurance Agents) in New York. The committee now had a clear project orientation, and was renamed as ACORD, with the acronym originally representing Agency-Company Operations Research and Development.

The first two words ("Agency-Company") show us the group is born out of relationships between different players. The inclusion of "Operations" shows the group was to be focused on how things get done between those parties. The "Research and Development" element of the name places a responsibility for solutions on to the group. This wasn't meant to be a talking-shop without substance, but an ongoing project that would work at the difficult meeting point between different commercial actors and their diverse methods of working. NAIA's 1972/3 ACORD brochure stressed the interlocking

> "ACORD stressed the interlocking nature of practicality and participation."

nature of practicality and participation, a theme that remains constant for the organization thirty-five years later:

> "The basic concept behind the project is that, because of the interrelated nature of many of these operating problems, practical solutions can only be effectively developed when all parties concerned actively participate in the development of the solutions."

ACORD's objective was easily stated in business terms: to simplify paperwork and procedures in order to reduce the day-to-day operating costs of both agencies and companies. Art Blum, President of the NAIA, acknowledged ACORD was "one of the most ambitious projects ever undertaken by the NAIA." Thirty-three major property and casualty insurance companies, along with the State Association Committees, participated: an unprecedented level of sustained co-operation.

The first public deliverable produced by ACORD was "a new uniform and simplified claim reporting procedure and forms for the industry." It was this package that first bore the ACORD name and

"ACORD standards could be applied neutrally throughout the industry."

logo. The emphasis was on ACORD standards as tried and tested products that could be applied neutrally throughout the industry. The new claims procedure was recognized as an industry first. But even in this first standard, Blum and his colleagues recognized the greater value of the standard's bigger message to the industry — and to the future:

> "We are proud of this accomplishment not only for its value to our industry, but as an excellent example of how agents and companies working together can find mutually beneficial solutions while providing greater value and better service to the insuring public. [...] We are looking forward to many more significant developments from the Project..."

From these earliest days, ACORD was organizationally light on its feet, with the bulk of the development effort coming from the participating organizations with the facilitation of one full-time project director. The rationale behind the group's work was the belief that practical recommendations for changes could only follow from a proper understanding of business requirements. The group was directed towards improvements in both efficiency and effectiveness, and was expected to "provide both agencies and companies with assistance in their use and adoption of accepted guidelines." ACORD was designed to be an implementer as well as a creator of standards.

Notably, business areas where competitive differentiators applied were excluded from the group's scope. These areas included "underwriting programs, coverages, pricing [and the] internal company management policy of agencies."

The original thirty-three participating companies were: Aetna, Aetna Life & Casualty, AID, Argonaut, Bituminous, Chubb, CNA, Commercial Union, Continental, Crum & Forster, Employers Mutual, Fireman's Fund, General Accident, Great American, Gulf Group, The Hartford, The Home, INA, Kemper, Maryland Casualty, New Hampshire, Northwestern National, Reliance, Royal-Globe, SAFECO, St. Paul, Statesman Group, Transamerica, Travelers, Unigard Group, USF&G, Westfield and Zurich-American.

The NAIA Agency-Company Study Committee was comprised of Chuck Liddle, Chairman (New York), Bob Newell (Illinois), Charles Bundy (Maryland), Louis Follis (Connecticut), Marvin Kristin (California), Gerald TeBockhorst (NAIA Committee), Don Perrin (NAIA Staff Administrator) and William F. Smith, Consultant to the Committee from Fireman's Fund Insurance Companies. The Project leader was W. Rodney Smith and the Assistant Project Leader was Charles J. Kriss.

ACORD was separated from the NAIA in 1975. It became a separate legal entity with its own bylaws and board of directors. The change was made to provide greater balance and neutrality to governance, and to involve more industry organizations.

Paper Forms

The needless redundancy in industry processes took a strikingly visible form in the 1970s: paper. Similar – but different – forms were being issued by insurers for use by agencies, and they were proliferating. This wasn't only a procedural headache for the players involved: from the point of view of the industry as a whole, it was a massive waste of money. ACORD was determined to eliminate the duplication, simplify the processes and save everybody time and money.

This was the first sign of what became a major grassroots effort to improve service to consumers, eliminate waste and lower the cost of doing business. Although ACORD was not originally created to focus on standardizing paper forms alone, it was a far more tractable task than dealing with the associated processes. Paper is tangible. It's hard to ignore. It takes up space, and it has to be handled. It serves as a direct connection between a process and its cost. Fast-forward to the new millennium, when so much of our paper has disappeared, and ponder this: if your organization was forced to print and manually file every single one of its emails, wouldn't people suddenly discover much of the email they create has no business value?

ACORD's concerted attack on paper forms also provided a clear focus for working committees. At one point we attempted to standardize direct (insurer) bill procedures for all insurers, because the differences were confusing for agency personnel. ACORD never did succeed in standardizing direct bill, but it did publish a direct bill manual to identify the differences in a standard way. This was an early indication that ACORD's work would inevitably expand in the years to come, unless other industry organizations emerged to carry out the work. The demands and opportunities generated by automation were not going to disappear.

NAIA's unwavering commitment to the ACORD Project led to a growing industry acceptance of its mission, particularly in light of the steady encroachment of direct writing insurers whose process was made less cumbersome by employing captive agents.

ACORD moved from its original home at NAIA headquarters in New York City, to Stamford, Connecticut before returning to Manhattan in 1973. Bob Merriman was brought in as Executive Director from Allstate and Johnson & Higgins and helmed ACORD from the famous Chrysler building on 42nd and Lexington.

With its assault on paper, ACORD was sensibly tackling the big, dumb problems first. The group's first initiatives on the process side were similarly practical, and visible. When an industry's workflow is mostly on paper, its most visible processes involve the handling or marking of paper. And there was no more potent symbol of the processing of paper than... the rubber stamp. One of ACORD's first process initiatives was a standard claims stamp used to record specific data on claim forms received by insurers. Early process initiatives also included a direct bill-processing manual to standardize procedures around the various direct bill systems being deployed by insurers.

Many of the process initiatives had a necessarily limited shelf life. However, the introduction of standard forms became the foundation for a substantial change in how we move, store and exploit information. The first standard insurance forms took several years to create and refine. They had to be tested in key states, and they had to be accepted by key influencers. ACORD was dealing with state insurance departments and state associations and also a large group of insurers. As the claim forms began to creep into the standard workflow of the industry, ACORD began work on standards for Binder, Certificate of Insurance and Notice of Cancellation. As today, the work was done by agency and insurer volunteers together with the ACORD staff at meetings convened and often hosted by member organizations.

From the outset, new business applications were off-limits to ACORD. Unlike administrative forms, which come to life after a sale, the information used to underwrite was viewed as the soul of the business. Management viewed their role as increasing differentiation and decreasing loss ratios. Nor did they make a distinction between moving data and acting upon it. Nevertheless, the leaders of ACORD were determined to standardize new business applications and they hired me from Chubb to lead the project in 1977.

"They viewed the standards as an avenue to increase revenue as part of an "ease of doing business" campaign.'' And since the independent agency distribution channel represented the market for the insurers, marketing executives became involved in ACORD. They viewed the standards not only as a means of lowering the cost in a multi-insurer distribution channel, but also as an avenue to increase revenue as part of an "ease of doing business" campaign. Sounds familiar, doesn't it? We began to develop commercial lines forms since this represented the path of least resistance among the EDP (Electronic Data Processing) crowd. Insurers had by now been automating personal lines policy processing for a few years.

Today, ACORD maintains 550 standard forms used by tens of thousands of agents and insurers. The program saves the industry tens of millions of dollars each year. Those savings are made up of the hard dollars previously used to generate redundant forms, and soft dollars associated with improving the workflow. Using simple arithmetic, if all the insurers developed, maintained and distributed their proprietary forms among agencies, the cost would be staggering. The same is true in the digital world, though less obvious than in the paper world.

The Electronic Dawn

Standard paper forms for agencies are only a small part of the insurance ecosystem. In contrast, data standards for moving information electronically are much more pervasive as a result of industry automation. As the standard paper forms were taking hold, some agents and insurers were looking at ways to create standards for moving information electronically.

The movement met with resistance by some insurers, who, quite reasonably, could not see any immediate benefits to themselves. However, agents were in the throes of a massive expansion in insurer systems that made the earlier generation's proliferation of paper forms look almost benign. At least paper is reasonably plentiful and doesn't suddenly go blank while you're using it. Nor do different shapes or sizes of paper require their readers to go on training courses. Paper isn't choosy about air-conditioning, and it isn't surrounded by a tribe of well-intentioned but often incomprehensible technical experts.

Insurers were busily installing their workstations in agencies, and every insurer had their own flavor. Some had been given creative names like the Continental's "Time Machine." The devices did offer benefits: they allowed agents to key data directly into insurer systems for new business and endorsements. But the downside was the workstations did not connect with the agency management system, so agents had to re-key data locally if they had their own system. From the insurer perspective, many agencies were not automated and used batch service bureaus for accounting, so connectivity and compatibility did not seem like a big problem. But it was already obvious the number of agency systems would increase as agencies brought more of their computing needs in-house.

Some agencies began to decline insurer workstation installations. To the horror of the insurers, the systems they had developed to help the agencies had become destroyers of business. Momentum was now building to resolve the front-end data management problem. Agencies wanted to eliminate redundant data entry and insurers wanted to find a better way to move data electronically from the agency.

> **"Agencies wanted to eliminate redundant data entry and insurers wanted to find a better way to move data electronically from the agency."**

A Network of Our Own

Since ACORD insurer members opposed expansion into electronic data standards, a splinter group of insurers and associations underwrote a study by the Stanford Research Institute (SRI) on the automation of the agency system. The study concluded, perhaps unsurprisingly, automation of the agency system was not only inevitable, but that standards would be essential for success and the creation of an industry-owned telecommunications network was timely.

In the days before telecoms deregulation in the mid-1980s and then the emergence of the public Internet after 1993, telecommunications networks were scarce, expensive and protected by technical, commercial and legislative hurdles. Shifting data along the public networks was a minority interest considered the proper preserve of only the largest organizations. Some of these created so-called Value Added Networks (VANs) that aggregated smaller organizations who wished to swap data with each other. General Electric and IBM were leading lights in this industry. The SRI study was, essentially, recommending the insurance industry create and operate its own VAN.

As a result, the Insurance Institute for Research (IIR) was born. The new organization would focus exclusively on electronic data processing and telecommunications. Irv Kelson was hired from IBM to be its first President. Initially about ten insurers joined the new organization and membership grew only slowly in the following years. In 1979, John Folk, the former President and CEO of Reliance Insurance Company, was named President of IIR.

IIR's early years were chaotic. The organization was at the bleeding edge of both technological and commercial development. With hindsight, it's easy to see the world needed deregulated telecoms markets and open networking standards. Although the blueprints for these developments already existed in different forms in the United States, Europe and Asia, their political time had not yet come. By contrast, ACORD's beginnings amongst the paper heaps of American agencies looks like a less risky, if less glamorous, environment for a cooperative industry body. IIR also had to cope with diverse interests and market drivers, as well as different concepts of how the world of connectivity would develop. The organization's board focused on three industry initiatives: a long-distance telephone discount program, electronic data standards, and an industry network facility.

A contract was negotiated with MCI to aggregate long-distance traffic, the discounts being shared by participants in the program. IIR also aggregated data traffic among participating insurers and negotiated a contract with IBM/IN (Information Network) in Tampa, Florida. And since EDI (Electronic Data Interchange) was expanding in other industries, the IIR was eager to establish data standards for moving insurance information.

There was some hope the cost of developing EDI (electronic data interchange) standards could be financed from network traffic revenue, but this never came to be. Instead, IIR approached ACORD. The standard insurance forms ACORD had created would not only facilitate the development of EDI standards but also accelerate the process. And that's exactly what happened.

ACORD and IIR formed a Joint Standards Committee in 1980, bringing together participants from each organization. The ACORD staff concentrated on the data requirements while the IIR staff handled the more technical aspects of the joint venture. The arrangement played to the strengths of each partner. ACORD staff members were assigned to work at the IIR office in White Plains, New York.

The Joint Standards Committee was extremely successful in setting EDI standards based on ACORD standard forms. The initiative was widely publicized and applauded. The initiative's public acclaim reinforced the practical strategy of morphing standard forms into data streams. The process wasn't simple, and we took some wrong turns. But we were building a highway others could follow. The marriage of standard forms and EDI worked because the forms were based on rigorous analysis of the requirements of the participating businesses. The forms were, in the paper technology of their time, the best physical representation of the industry's fundamental data constructs. EDI offered a means of dematerializing the paper, leaving the data structure intact.

Regrouping for Standards

The success of the Joint Standards Committee made it clear ACORD and IIR should become one organization. ACORD had about seventy-five members in contrast to IIR's twenty members, but all IIR members were also members of ACORD. And it was obvious to many, ACORD should have undertaken the EDI standards work in the first place.

The most difficult part of the merger negotiations related to the future of the IIR industry network. This network was named IVANS (Insurance Value Added Network Services). ACORD members were concerned their membership dollars were going to finance an industry network that competed with other networks — including private networks owned by some of the major insurers. Therefore, when IIR and ACORD merged in 1983, it was agreed IVANS would be separated from IIR/ACORD and become an entity financed by its own subscribers.

The newly merged IIR/ACORD was to focus exclusively on the promulgation of EDI data standards. John Folk, President of IIR became President of IIR/ACORD as well as President of IVANS. ACORD's CEO Bob Merriman became Executive Vice President of the new IIR/ACORD organization. On Folk's retirement, Bob Barham (formerly IBM) was named President of IVANS and Bob Merriman became CEO of IIR/ACORD after Joseph Quinn, an interim CEO, had left.

ACORD closed its office, which by now was in Oradell, New Jersey, and relocated to the new IIR/ACORD office in White Plains, New York. After a few years, the organization's title was trimmed back to the simpler name of ACORD. In 1990, ACORD moved to Pearl River, New York to be near the Insurance Services Office (ISO).

ACORD and ISO shared forms distribution facilities, so the relocation saved the organization time and money.

Bob Merriman retired in 1994, and I was elected President by the ACORD board of directors that year. At the same time, deep and widespread changes in the industry brought about significant growth at ACORD. The membership now included many financial services firms operating globally. We continued to support the independent agencies, as we do today, but acquired a wider field of vision for industry standards to meet the needs of an expanding and changing membership. This expansion has never detracted from the original agency focus; but insurers can always use more reasons to implement data standards across their organizations. Moving information efficiently was now a much larger objective, and one that clearly benefited everybody.

Life and Annuity

We expanded ACORD's standards to include life and (L&A) in 1996 by assuming the work started by SLIEC (Solutions for Life Insurance Enterprise Computing), an ad hoc industry group of insurers and vendors. I met with SLIEC's Planning Committee and together we drafted a proposal for review by the ACORD Board of Directors.

Our Board realized standards needed to transcend lines of business. The P&C (property & casualty also know as "non life") insurers understood this as well, but their interests were more parochial and they were concerned about resources.

"Standards have naturally gravitated towards ACORD."

ACORD L&A standards ultimately included the original data standards created by NAILBA (National Association of Independent Life Brokerage Agencies). NAILBA, like many trade associations, became involved in data standards to address the data transfer needs of their membership. The ongoing development and implementation of standards is not necessarily something a trade body can do on its own without diverting resources from its core responsibilities. Standards have naturally gravitated towards ACORD, and this process of consolidation has steadily improved the reach, quality and economic impact of the organization's work.

Reinsurance

Meanwhile, other organizations had been busy creating data standards for reinsurance. Reinsurance data is of course closely related to the data types covered by the core ACORD standards, so rather than work at cross-purposes, we decided to work closely with these organizations. After all, the data being passed from the policyholder to the agent or from the broker to the insurer is essentially the same in both insurance and reinsurance.

We, therefore began working in the late 1990s with WIN (World Insurance Network), RINET (Reinsurance Network) and LIMNET (The London Market Network). These bodies all merged to become a single organization named WISe (World Insurance Services).

WISe was also involved in the Joint Venture (JV) that had created some basic reinsurance standards, including a set of back-office reinsurance accounting standards being used by RINET in Brussels. Other members of the joint venture included IVANS, the BRMA (Broker Reinsurance Markets Association) and the RAA (Reinsurance Association of America).

Although WISe had been involved in standards-setting through the JV, its main tasks were operating a network and building a secure email and document exchange service dubbed Trusted Trading. Originally a WIN creation, the Trusted Trading platform did not have much take-up among brokers and insurers for a number of reasons. Part of the problem was the emergence of the Internet diverting attention to less costly and potentially more innovative ways to exchange information that had not been available when the platform was originally conceived. WISe looked for guidance to other industries such as banking and brokerage that had successfully created standards and aggregated transactions through industry-owned clearing houses. However, the complexity of the insurance process and the heavy data payloads involved made it difficult to replicate those simpler models.

With the advice of management consultants Bain & Company, it became obvious WISe would find it hard to be both a neutral standards-setting body and a purveyor of technology solutions. The two objectives ran counter to each other, and undermined the organization's rationale. The joint venture was also running out of steam after creating a few EDI message types and completing a small number of implementations. The reinsurance standards not only needed to be separated from the commercial venture at WISe, but also become part of a larger industry initiative including related lines of significant commercial business with many more industry players. ACORD's large footprint in the business and success with attracting participants and facilitating implementations did not go unnoticed by the leaders of WISe.

After a year or two of working with WISe, the synergies of consolidating the standards became a topic of discussion. In 2001, the WISe board of directors (chaired by Rob White-Cooper of Marsh) and the ACORD board of directors (chaired by John Leonard of MEMIC), agreed to merge the WISe standards into ACORD. ACORD hired some of the WISe staff in Brussels and London and the members of WISe automatically became members of ACORD. Around twenty organizations joined ACORD via WISe, including AON, Generali, Lloyd's of London, Marsh, Munich Re, SCOR, Swiss Re, and Willis. In July of 2001, ACORD opened a London office at the London Underwriting Centre.

The History of Our Future

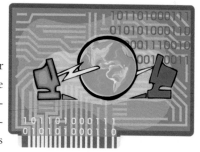

The Internet has been a major catalyst for ACORD standards in recent years. In the past, it was a major problem just to get computers talking to each other. But connectivity is no longer an issue today, and focus has shifted to the need to move information in real time and seamlessly among all trading partners. Asking customers, distributors, suppliers or partners to exchange information in a proprietary format or by using a proprietary system is increasingly unacceptable in today's business environment. The emergence of XML (eXtensible Markup Language) offers us the means to tag data with the simplicity and flexibility developers found so elusive through the years. This is truly a new world unfolding before our eyes.

"Focus has shifted to the need to move information in real time and seamlessly."

Doing business is becoming increasingly dependent on stable and reliable insurance industry-specific standards. And to achieve this, ACORD is committed to work with all the standards organizations across the globe to harmonize, converge or build standards in partnership on behalf of our collective members.

While less is more when it comes to standards, a single global standard to support all business in all parts of the world is not a practical vision. Therefore, developing standards with other groups that can interconnect and sharing data models that can support both global and local business requirements is our vision.

> **"ACORD members can migrate from one technology to the next as new solutions come along."**

ACORD Standards will not only support all lines of business and span the globe, but remain industry-owned and technology (platform) neutral. And this means ACORD members can migrate from one technology to the next as new solutions come along.

Standards not only allow us to send, receive, share and exchange data electronically, they also take competitive strategy to a new level. And our job at ACORD is to help you do so successfully. We now provide standards for property and casualty, life and annuity, surety and reinsurance lines of business and our members come from all parts of the world.

ACORD was born to be a focal point in a complex network of relationships. Its first incarnation was at the meeting-point of agents and insurers, and its early mission was focused on keeping this meeting-point clear and functioning smoothly. As the years have gone by, and as legions of volunteers have built out ACORD standards and implemented them in the field, it has become ever clearer that a multi-player industry as vital as ours needs an organization that will act as an interface amongst all the others. The goals of industry players may change, and their relationships with each other develop and mutate. Yet there is a constant need to move information amongst them. And the fundamental economics of moving information have not changed since the pioneers at ACORD declared war on the paper snowdrifts.

Over one thousand insurers representing all segments of the business, more than two hundred major solution providers and most of the industry trade associations participate in ACORD today. And we continue to talk about ACORD's role of bringing the industry together, because that's precisely what our founders expect us to do.

References

1 Berkley Books, New York, 1999

2 Carlota Perez, *Technological revolutions and financial capital: the dynamics of bubbles and golden ages*, Edward Elgar, 2002

3 From *The Economist*, May 8, 2003

4 Charles Spurgeon, *Ethernet: the definitive guide*, O'Reilly, 2000, quoted in *The Economist*, May 24, 2003

5 http://www.business2.com/articles/mag/0,1640,37613,00.html

6 HarperBusiness, 2002

7 Samuel L. Macey, *The Dynamics of Progress: Time, Method, and Measure*, 1990, University of Georgia Press, p71

8 ibid, p73

9 Though the US currency fudges the pure decimal system by having a "quarter" piece. This is a remnant of the pre-revolutionary currency environment, where Spanish reals ("pieces of eight") were the de facto standard and the slicing of coins was common. (The expression "two bits" is another remnant of the wilder days of coins.)

10 The British are not fully "harmonized" with the rest of Europe. Brits accept the liter as a measure for gasoline, but cling to the mile as the measure of their car journeys. (And the mile? One thousand Roman soldier paces.)

11 IEEE, http://www.thinkstandards.net/benefits.html

12 Jason Goodwin, *Greenback: The almighty dollar and the invention of America*, Hamish Hamilton, 2003, p129

13 http://www.adage.com/news.cms?newsId=34950

14 http://www.aft.org/stand/previous/1993/082993.html

15 Andrew Summers, "In my opinion." *Management Today*, May 2003.

16 Joseph L. Bower and Clayton M. Christensen, "Disruptive Technologies: Catching the Wave." *Harvard Business Review* Article #95103, January 1995. http://harvardbusinessonline.hbsp.harvard.edu/b01/en/common/item_detail.jhtml?id=95103

17 *Megaprojects and Risk*, Bent Flyvbjerg, Cambridge University Press, quoted in *Prospect*, April 2003

18 http://www.cssinfo.com/whystandards.html

19 If you answered "Practice!" go to the back of the class. Carnegie Hall comes later.

20 Simon & Schuster, 1990

21 ibid

22 James Randerson, "Traffic plan for Venice rules the waves." *New Scientist*, September 27, 2003

23 Peter Schwartz, Peter Leyden, Joel Hyatt, *The Long Boom: A Vision for the Coming Age of Prosperity*

24 Peter Schwartz, *Inevitable Surprises: Thinking Ahead in a Time of Turbulence*, Gotham Books, 2003; p84

25 Novelist George Eliot (Mary Ann Evans) (1819-80).

26 *The New York Times*, 1897

27 Figures from Anthony Markel in a speech to the Insurance Institute of London, March 16, 2004; quoted in *Eye of the Market*:1 ….
[complete ref]

Index